Weird

BUT

NORMAL

Weird

= BUT =

NORMAL

ESSAYS

MIA MERCADO

HarperOne
An Imprint of HarperCollinsPublishers

HarperOne

Illustrations on pages 5 (*top*) and 169 (*top*): Fafarumba | Shutterstock
Illustrations on pages 5 (*bottom*), 67, 117 (*top*), 169 (*bottom*), and 215:
mspoint | VectorStock
Illustration on page 117 (*bottom*): nikiteev_konstantin | Shutterstock

Photograph on page 263 courtesy of Chase Castor.

Versions of the following essays were previously published online:
"White Friend Confessional" on McSweeney's Internet Tendency;
"I'm a Guy's Girl" on NewYorker.com's Daily Shouts; "Bath & Body
Works Is the Suburban Nonsense I Crave" on BUST.com; "A Nice
Piece of Satire You Can Take Home to Your Parents" on Belladonna
Comedy, thebelladonnacomedy.com.

HarperCollins books may be purchased for educational, business,
or sales promotional use. For information, please email the Special
Markets Department at SPsales@harpercollins.com.

FIRST EDITION

Designed by Janet Evans-Scanlon

Library of Congress Cataloging-in-Publication Data has been applied for.

ISBN 978-0-06-294280-7

20 21 22 23 24 LSC 10 9 8 7 6 5 4 3 2 1

For you, mostly,
and a little bit
for me

CONTENTS

PART V: ON BEING HUMAN

PREFACE/INTRO/I DON'T KNOW WHAT TO CALL THIS BUT IT'S LIKE

THIS IS WHAT THE BOOK IS ABOUT

PLEASE DON'T SKIM

OKAY YOU'RE SKIPPING IT ENTIRELY

NEVERMIND

I spend a lot of my time wondering what it would be like to feel normal all the time. To wake up, refreshed, after exactly eight hours of sleep and walk through life feeling confident and self-assured. To breathe in the new day and think, "I bet everyone I encounter will want to hear what I have to say." Never stopping to wonder, "Maybe my third-grade teacher hated me and I didn't know?" To fall asleep so, so easily, never worrying about the dumb thing I said earlier that day or the dumb thing I might say tomorrow or the dumb thing I said in Sunday school a decade ago.

I don't think anyone feels completely normal all of the time, but I do feel like I've spent much of my life being highly embarrassed by my body, my brain, and my whole entire self. I am wildly comfortable with being uncomfortable in my own skin.

I've tried to wax, pluck, cleanse, ignore, self-care, ironically joke about, and self-deprecatingly tweet the discomfort away, and wow, can you believe it, the feeling of not feeling normal has never actually left me.

This is not to ignore the many cis, straight, able-bodied privileges I have been afforded. I know checking one's privilege has become an empty rallying cry for anyone who wants to talk about the intersection of the personal and the political. Often, I wonder whether I'm different enough to have any authority on the subject of feeling strange. If my face passes as white when my summer tan fades. If my brain passes as healthy when I don't talk about my depression. But it would be a lie to ignore the ways in which I'm constantly reminded I'm different. Being out of place feels as normal to me as the air we all breathe.

My discomfort with those differences has led me to preemptively tell everyone all the ways in which I assume I'm strange. (Would Defense Mechanism be a good name for an emo band?) I've thought, "Maybe if I tokenize my half-Asian self in this wholly white room, one of the multiple Megans will not do it to me." Or, "Perhaps I can fill my Twitter feed with these deeply negative feelings and each Like will give me one (1) serotonin." But, oops surprise, talking about hating yourself does not a personality make. It isn't a fun, quirky brand of comedy. It's just really draining. And ultimately, sad.

So, I'm trying this thing where I acknowledge the parts of myself that make me feel weird without quantifying them as "bad." Because, oops surprise again, a lot of the parts of ourselves we assume to be strange are actually really common. Despite the dozens of bottles I've bought since 2001, I cannot be the only person keeping Nair in the hair-removal business. Because I have eyes and ears and a Wi-Fi connection, I know I am not the only one screaming for the world to love them while also tweeting things like "lol @ that feeling when ur just a big trash dump!!!"

These parts of ourselves are often internalized and intentionally hidden. They're associated with shame, guilt, and panic dreams where Sarah from Catholic confirmation class tells everyone, "Mia thinks premarital sex is bad, but joke's on her because she is years out from seeing even one single penis!" If we talked about these awkward parts more, we'd realize many of the things we think make us weird are astonishingly normal.

While we're obsessing about things that are actually quite ordinary, there are lots of legitimately strange things we should be directing our time, tweets, and energy toward. Weird things we've come to culturally accept as normal, like expecting women to wear uncomfortable shoes that make them taller—but not so tall as to scare straight men; how we shave some body hair while conditioning others; and the fact that we light a cake on fire and sing to it to celebrate being alive. Sometimes all I want to do is rip off my BOGO heels and scream, "WHAT IS EVEN GOING ON HERE?"

There are rituals, specifically those of womanhood, that I follow blindly, only pausing briefly to contemplate why I think I need a $25 candle that smells like an ocean that doesn't exist. Going on a Target run makes me feel seen on a spiritual level, and I have, more than once, eaten Halo Top ice cream and called it self-care. I am not above admittedly absurd, ritualistic ways of living. I am deeply in the trenches of them, holding my breath and trying to make eye contact with someone else down here who shares my discomfort with the whole situation.

I know I don't have all or perhaps any of the answers when it comes to feeling normal in our weird human flesh. I don't know all the steps to freeing either the nipple or my increasing number of nipple hairs, but I do know that I can't keep up with all the tweezing, tittering, trimming, and shrinking socially required to be a "normal" human woman in this weird-ass world.

I'm fucking tired. At the end of the day, sometimes I just want to laugh. Or half-smile. Or do one of those appreciatory silently-blow-air-out-of-my-nose-but-not-really-laugh laughs. Maybe we can all exhale a little together.

Part 1

ON BEING

#Human™

These are stories about our outward-facing selves. The face we put on when we leave the house. The assumptions people make when they see that face. As much as I'd like to mask the ways in which I feel strange or uncomfortable or out of place, the world is going to see me however they see me. These are stories about people's assumptions about me because I'm half-Asian, half-white, from the Midwest, female, racially ambiguous, violently beautiful, aggressively charismatic, humble.

These are stories about how I've hidden behind the people I've pretended to be and the people I'm expected to be, how I often feel I'm performing normality rather than just living it. They're about the fact that these are all standard practices of being a person.

I AM THE GIRL FROM
YOUR TAMPON COMMERCIALS

Everyone starts out strange. As children, we're all just tiny, little weirdos testing the limits of what is normal, acceptable behavior and what makes our parents blush or swear in public. "But *I* wasn't a strange child," you say, actively blocking out memories where you shoved bundled up socks down your pants or played a made-up game called Dead Girl where the whole premise was that you were a girl who was dead. I promise you, all children are fucking weird.

When I was little but not little enough for it to be cute (nine or ten-ish), I used to play a game called Orphans with my sister and cousins who were all five to seven years younger than me. The game went like this: we were orphans trying to escape an orphanage. That's it. That was the whole game. I think I saw *Annie* once and let it become my entire personality for most of elementary school.

When playing the classic game Orphans, you start by making up orphan names and identities. I, the oldest and therefore bossiest/bitchiest of the group, took to writing down each of our names and personas in a notebook. This was the majority of the game. My sister, whose non-orphan name is Ana, would be a Jessica or Stephanie or Cassandra. My cousins would be a Stephanie or Cassandra or Jessica, depending on who Ana didn't want to be. I would almost always be Molly, a brunette with freckles.

I could have been Esther, a fairy trapped in a human girl's body, or Indigo, an alien with three-foot eyelashes, or even Debra, a bucket with arms and legs. But my dream Orphan Girl was Molly, a brunette with freckles.

That, I suppose, was the epitome of a "pretty girl" to me, as someone who was/is/always will be half-Asian, half-white, and wholly racially ambiguous.* My hair is technically brown. I do have these faint, freckle-adjacent things dotted around my eyes and nose. But no one has or will ever describe me as "a brunette with freckles."

The thing about racial ambiguity is it is never self-assigned. You first dip a toe in it when you don't know what racial box to check on a form. (Who gets to claim "Other" in the Race Wars???) You wade in further still when someone makes a comment about *those* people in front of you, a member of *those* implied people. You realize you've been completely drenched this whole time after enough people ask, "What *are* you?" In those moments, you wish you were Debra, a bucket with arms and legs.

One of the first times I realized the world had dubbed me "ambiguous," I was about eight and in a library in suburban

---

* Though I was still too young then to be fully actualized about my race, I knew girls, even orphaned ones, were most important when pretty.

Wisconsin. My family had come for a free children's program where someone from the zoo brought in animals. This was both so kids could learn about animals and so parents could pretend their kids were learning about animals while they could have one goddamn brief moment of peace. After showing off snakes and various bugs for kids to *ooh* and *ugh* at, the speaker brought out his grand finale: a porcupine.

"Who wants to come feed the porcupine a banana?" the animal man asked, like it was a normal thing to say. In a rare moment of extroversion, I raised my hand. He called me up, and I made my way through the small group of kids seated cross-legged on the floor. He asked me my name. I said, "Mia." He asked where I was from. I said, "Glendale," the small city outside of Milwaukee where I'd lived my entire life. It was also the place where the library and, in turn, all of us were currently located. "No," he asked again, probably chuckling a little, "Where are you *from*?"

Now, in my late twenties, I'm all too familiar with this line of questioning. The little laugh that comes along with the change in emphasis, like *I'm* the dum-dum for not realizing how racially unidentifiable my face is. "What ethnicity are you?" or a question along similar misinformed lines is something I've been asked so frequently my answer is not only well-rehearsed, it comes equipped with a brief lesson in Filipino history and the etymology of my last name. I'm working on a choreographed musical number called, "Spain Colonized the Philippines and All I Got Was a Spanish-Sounding Last Name and a Whole Lot of Catholicism."

My dad is Filipino; he came to the US at sixteen. My mom is white, most likely German and Irish and sometimes she throws in something spicy and exotic like French. Despite what "multicultural" marketing campaigns would have you believe, our house was not some bicultural mecca, equal and distinct parts Filipino and white. Sometimes we'd eat chicken adobo and I'd hear my dad talk to his siblings on the phone in Tagalog. We also ate a lot of cream cheese and saw my mom's side of the family for most holidays. My siblings and I frequently asked my dad things like "How do you say 'pass the juice'?" (*Paki abot ng juice*) and "Do we have accents to you?" (*No*). That was the extent to which any of us questioned our own race.

At eight, I hadn't given much thought to being biracial, let alone being "racially ambiguous." So, when a man I'd just met with a porcupine I'd also just met asked where I was from, for a second time, I simply replied, ". . . America?" I was about to feed a banana to a porcupine in a public library in Wisconsin, and somehow I was the most foreign part of the situation. I'm sure he laughed at my naivety. I wish I would have laughed at his.

I've learned my assumed race changes depending on where I am. When my family moved to an even more suburban town in Wisconsin, one I now know has a population that is about 97 percent white, people thought I was Chinese.

When other kids, and adults for that matter, would call me Chinese, I didn't really understand the nuance, but I knew they weren't trying to start a dialogue about race. Could you imagine, though? Me and A.J., two nine-year-olds from Grafton, Wisconsin, having a thoughtful discussion on the sociopolitical implications of race and not being white in America? Mrs. G asking if my lack of participation in class was influenced by my assumptions about being female, being Asian, or both? I couldn't even articulate why the Blue Power Ranger was my favorite. I obviously was not about to talk eloquently about race with anyone. (In hindsight, I realize it was because Billy, the Blue Power Ranger, made me the horniest.)

Sometimes people would identify me as Chinese, but like a question rather than a statement. As if they knew they shouldn't be assigning my ethnicity to me but couldn't keep themselves from blurting it out. "You're . . . *Chi* . . . *nese* . . . ?" they'd say, waiting for me to confirm or disagree or clap or laugh or, perhaps, implode entirely.

This is about the time when I met my friend Racial Ambiguity. We'll call her Rachel, for short. We're on a first-name basis, me and her.

Rachel was cool! Rachel was mysterious! Rachel was my best and closest friend!!! Being Racially Ambiguous™ (cue rainbows and sparkles) was my exit ramp from being seen as Exclusively Asian/Chinese/LOL ARE THEY EVEN DIFFERENT THOUGH HA HA WAIT WHERE ARE YOU GOING?

Rachel and I lived in our own post-racial world. We took it as a compliment when people assumed I and the only other Asian kid in my graduating high school class were either dating or related (it was actually neither!!!). We bragged to our friends senior year when Blake, a decidedly hot boy, called *us* hot!!! Leaving out the part where he said, "for an Asian girl." When other people got yearbook superlatives like Most Likely to Succeed and Most Likely to Get Arrested (2008 in suburban Wisconsin was weird), we obliged when our friend said I looked like Brenda Song and agreed to have my face on the Celebrity Look-Alike page. I guess, if you think about it, my superlative was

Most Asian. Rachel and I suppressed that memory from middle school when two girls we didn't know called me a "monkey" at the public pool. We tried not to think about how that happened the summer when our skin was darker and we hadn't yet learned about Nair for Facial Hair. Rachel Ambiguity was my best, most delusional friend.

College was similar. Rachel and I either believed ourselves to be white-passing enough for people to say nothing or we ignored race altogether. I realize this is a strange sort of privilege, to not feel an urgency to confront your half-whiteness. To have your ethnicity seen as "exotic" instead of overtly threatening. To have the racism you experience be coded instead of explicit. This is not meant to be an excuse for the undeniably awful things people have said to and about me. It is, hopefully, a bit of consolation to some other biracial kid out there, staring at themselves in the mirror, playing the "Which parts of my face are Asian and which are white?" game. The answer is all of them are both.

The first time I felt Seen™ was a 2010 Kotex commercial. It showed a "believably attractive, eighteen- to twenty-four-year-old female" walking confidently around an all-white set. "You can relate to me because I'm racially ambiguous," the actress said, cheekily. *Yes*, Rachel and I whispered, staring at this facsimile of our own unidentifiable features, *we relate*.

I remember a flood of Othering moments. A catalog of times I ignored my own differences, hoping it'd make them disappear to everyone else. But it hadn't stopped that guy in high school who, when we were out bowling with our friends, wrote my name down as "rice picker" on the TV screen that keeps score. It didn't stop someone from shouting, "Asians are gay! I hate Asians!" as

I walked home from babysitting one evening.* It didn't stop a girl during my senior year of high school from playfully talking about how she wished she could "borrow" my skin for scholarship applications.

After going to college, based solely on the color of my skin, of course, I moved to Kansas City for a job. There, I magically became a proud Latina woman! My first day as a full-time employee, I was included on an email with a handful of other people, asking about our experiences with quinceañeras. (I had never had one nor been to one.) When my team was developing products specifically targeted toward Asian American consumers—yes, the word used is "target"; the thing about corporate America is it is often extremely gross and disgusting!—I offered my opinion. Saying I was ignored is almost being generous. I'm assuming I wasn't "Asian enough" or "the right kind of Asian" or, as they likely would have put it, not within their "target demographic" (AKA I wasn't Asian enough). In one meeting, comprised of about ten people, one of whom had "Vice President" in her title, people were talking about "Trends Among Hispanic Consumers" or some other euphemistic way to say "Oh, LOL, we should talk about Latinx people, huh?" The Vice President turned to me and said, "Do these insights resonate with you?"

I panicked, initially thinking she was calling me out on my "Has Good Ideas but Needs to Participate in Class More" vibe. That panic lasted about five seconds before I realized . . . this

---

* What I love about this is that it covers so, so many bigoted bases! Slur-based multitasking! So efficient! This is the #GirlBoss of Hateful Remarks and, in that regard, we must clap!

bitch who makes five times my salary is so confident that I am Latinx, she just asked me about it in a work meeting.

I did what any girl and her Racially Ambiguous aura would do in the situation: I took out my proverbial top hat and tap shoes and went into my "Oh, Actually I'm Asian" song and dance. I finished out strong with "It's Okay, a Lot of People Think Filipinos Are Latinx. You Aren't the First and Won't Be the Last (The White Audience Reprise)." I took a bow (probably literally because I'm Asian), and she giggled away any guilt. White female boomers breathily laughing away their racial biases is my personal version of white noise.

This was nothing new. My white maternal great-grandma, a woman I was related to by blood, thought my siblings and I were Cuban literally until she died. I remember my mom recounting stories in which she, a white woman, was out for a walk with me and my three siblings, all half-Asian, and passersby would ask, "Where did you get them?" I am far more familiar with being the only nonwhite face in a room than I am being around people who are Asian or even racially ambiguous. My identity was developed in the context of always, *always* being in the minority.

"How Asian do I look?" is a question I often ask the people closest to me even today. I used to stare at pictures of me and Ana, my younger sister, panicking about whether she looked "more white" than I did. This was, in hindsight, me panicking about me not being as pretty as her.* I now realize neither of us is particularly white-passing. We are both equally hot.

---

* The roots of internalized racism and sexism run deep, and they are sprinkled with the Miracle-Gro that is prioritizing "beauty" and pretending it equates to happiness.

Sometimes I check "Other" on forms that ask my race. While I've never just marked "White," sometimes I only mark "Asian." I still don't know if, in the hypothetical yet somehow seemingly imminent Race Wars, I will get to be Team Asian or Team Racially Ambiguous. Regardless, I know I am not Team Passably White.

I am, admittedly, still unlearning childhood reflexes. I know that Chinese and Asian are not one and the same, but I need to actively remind myself that neither is synonymous with "bad" or "ugly" or "you must know kung fu, right?" I hope, in the process, I don't unlearn every strange part of myself. The parts that are naive and not self-hating, the parts that are simultaneously innocent and knowing.

I don't feel an active need to separate myself from my parents, to choose White or Asian or Both or Neither. At least not all of the time. I no longer wish to be Molly, a brunette with freckles, at least not on a regular basis. I'm starting to be okay with being Mia. Hopefully, someday soon, everyone else will get there, too.

WHITE FRIEND CONFESSIONAL

WHITE FRIEND: Forgive me, Designated Friend of Color, for I have sinned. It has been two Macklemore singles since my last white confession.

FRIEND OF COLOR: Go on.

WHITE FRIEND: I maybe did a racist thing.

FRIEND OF COLOR: Did you say the N-word during karaoke again?

WHITE FRIEND: No! I was definitely tempted to do "Formation" by Beyoncé but did "Single Ladies" instead.

FRIEND OF COLOR: That's growth, I guess. What did you want to talk about then?

WHITE FRIEND: So, the other day I couldn't tell the difference between two Asian women. But that's not necessarily racist, right?

FRIEND OF COLOR: Who were the women?

WHITE FRIEND: Does it really matter?

FRIEND OF COLOR: Who were they?

WHITE FRIEND: I realized my mistake right after!

FRIEND OF COLOR: Who did you think you saw?

WHITE FRIEND: Constance Wu at Target.

FRIEND OF COLOR: We live in Topeka.

WHITE FRIEND: She could have been filming her show or something.

FRIEND OF COLOR: In Topeka? You know what, never mind. I was expecting it to be a lot worse.

WHITE FRIEND: Thank you. Also, that cashier looked just like her.

FRIEND OF COLOR: Are you talking about the cashier who's in her midsixties?

WHITE FRIEND: I don't know. Don't Asian people never age or something?

FRIEND OF COLOR: Explain the science on how that would work.

WHITE FRIEND: I'm joking. I've seen old Asian people before. They're adorable. If I saw one holding a baby, I'd die from the cuteness.

FRIEND OF COLOR: Babies are cute. That's basically their whole thing.

WHITE FRIEND: Especially Asian babies. Ugh, I wish I could have an Asian baby.

FRIEND OF COLOR: Was that all you wanted to tell me?

WHITE FRIEND: Oh and last month, I tweeted a joke about Trump's disaster of a Black History Month speech.

FRIEND OF COLOR: And?

WHITE FRIEND: I spelled Frederick Douglass's name wrong.

FRIEND OF COLOR: You forgot the second "s"?

WHITE FRIEND: And the second "e."

FRIEND OF COLOR: The important part is you remembered what he did.

WHITE FRIEND: . . .

FRIEND OF COLOR: You had to google it, didn't you?

WHITE FRIEND: I remembered immediately after I looked it up!

FRIEND OF COLOR: Your penance will be to read something by or about Frederick Douglass.

WHITE FRIEND: Does it count if I just retweet Ta-Nehisi Coates a couple times?

FRIEND OF COLOR: What? No.

WHITE FRIEND: But what if I quote-tweet it and put #BlackLivesMatter?

FRIEND OF COLOR: You can do that too, I guess. But also, read something about Frederick Douglass.

WHITE FRIEND: Oh, I actually already did!

FRIEND OF COLOR: Was it a satirical piece about Frederick Douglass that was actually about Trump?

WHITE FRIEND: Maybe.

FRIEND OF COLOR: I guess that's better than nothing.

WHITE FRIEND: Okay, good.

FRIEND OF COLOR: Anything else?

WHITE FRIEND: Wanna hear something so crazy?

FRIEND OF COLOR: I told you I don't want to hear about the number of people who aren't white you matched with on Tinder.

WHITE FRIEND: No, it's not that. But I do swipe right on a lot of black guys, and I even swiped right on a guy who's Chinese yesterday.

FRIEND OF COLOR: Did his bio say he's Chinese?

WHITE FRIEND: What?

FRIEND OF COLOR: Just tell me what you were going to say.

WHITE FRIEND: Someone asked me if I'm Hispanic the other day.

FRIEND OF COLOR: And?

WHITE FRIEND: That's it. I just wanted to tell you. Isn't that so crazy?

FRIEND OF COLOR: Why would that be crazy?

WHITE FRIEND: I don't know. I thought you'd appreciate it.

FRIEND OF COLOR: Because?

WHITE FRIEND: Because you're Hispanic?

FRIEND OF COLOR: . . .

WHITE FRIEND: Sorry, I mean Latina?

FRIEND OF COLOR: . . .

WHITE FRIEND: Half-Mexican?

FRIEND OF COLOR: I'm Filipino.

WHITE FRIEND: Oh my god, I'm so sorry. That was totally gonna be my next guess.

FRIEND OF COLOR: Don't worry about it. It's fine.

WHITE FRIEND: I feel so awful. I can't believe I did that.

FRIEND OF COLOR: It's okay. I've heard worse things.

WHITE FRIEND: Oh my god, that's so true. You probably get stuff like that all the time.

FRIEND OF COLOR: Yeah, it's basically routine at this point.

WHITE FRIEND: It just makes me so sad to know racism still exists. I get so upset when I hear about it. And here I go thinking you're Mexican! I'll never forgive myself.

FRIEND OF COLOR: You can donate to the ACLU as an act of contrition.

WHITE FRIEND: I'm already a card-carrying member, but I guess I can always give a little more this month.

FRIEND OF COLOR: Feel better?

WHITE FRIEND: So much. Thanks.

FRIEND OF COLOR: Of course. This confessional was built to make you feel better.

WHITE FRIEND: I'm so glad I can come to you for this kind of stuff.

FRIEND OF COLOR: I mean, I'm not an expert on all non-white people, but no problem.

WHITE FRIEND: Right, of course. It's still such a relief to know I'm not racist.

FRIEND OF COLOR: You know I can't actually absolve you of that, right?

WHITE FRIEND: You just did. See you next week!

THE HAPPIEST PLACE
ON EARTH, GOD DAMMIT

The year was 2003: scientists were obsessed with cloning animals, the US invaded Iraq and eventually captured Saddam Hussein, and I went to Disney World for the first and only time. It was a significant year for all of us.

When my family and I went to Disney World, I was deep in the throes of being twelve, almost thirteen, and didn't want to be around my family even a little bit. At least, I didn't want *to look* like it was something I wanted. This was the same summer I competed in a preteen beauty pageant, in case you needed further proof I was the most important thing in my life at the time.

I suppressed my excitement about going to Disney World, I'm sure. I probably told people I was more excited for my younger siblings to go because it'd be so fun for them. Not me, though. My taste was too sophisticated to care about teacup rides or meeting Mickey or general whimsy. I cared about real culture, like memorizing Avril Lavigne lyrics and wearing clothes that made it look like I knew how to skateboard.

I don't remember any part of the journey from Wisconsin to Florida. I'm sure traveling as a family of six was a nightmare I've managed to suppress deep, deep down in my brain next to where I keep my memories about having bangs. I know, at least in hindsight, that taking a family trip was a big deal. Most of our family vacations up until that point were going "camping" at my grandparents' house. They lived on a lake in Fond du Lac, Wisconsin, where all the grandkids spent summers cutting the shit out of our ankles on zebra mussels while jumping off the dock, getting yelled at by our parents for not wearing water shoes (a necessity for swimming in a lake), and sleeping in a tent in the yard and calling it "camping." That or we'd go to the amusement park in Green Bay that was affordable and where I barfed on a ride called the Scrambler, obviously.

In Florida, we arrived at the cabin where we'd be staying for the week—camping-themed things were big for us because they were usually less expensive. Eager to please and easily impressed, my siblings and I would gleefully eat a lukewarm hotdog outside or piss in a bush if we were told we were camping. I remember each of my three siblings and I getting "signed" pictures of whichever Disney character our parents had told the resort was our favorite. Mine was Jasmine. So, sitting on the cabin's kitchen table was a Sharpie'd autograph from whatever racially ambiguous nineteen-year-old got to pretend to be Jasmine that summer.

My affinity for Jasmine was/is complicated. A part of that love comes from my deep, deep horniness for Aladdin, the hottest Disney prince. (He wears a PURPLE VEST with NO SHIRT underneath it. He is a bad boi turned good boi. "A Whole New World" is an endlessly erotic song. "Unbelievable sights"? "Indescribable feelings"??? I'd continue but then I'd need to take a cold shower.) Another part of that love came from a deep, deep need to disassociate from Mulan, the more Asian princess.

It wasn't until college that I started desperately clinging to any small shred of Asian representation. (And I'm only now starting to grapple with the impulsive need to declare how "seen" I feel when Hollywood tosses me the slightest hint of Asianness or anytime someone whispers "Sandra Oh.") In middle school, I was most certainly trying to lean into racial ambiguity rather than anything overtly Asian, and Jasmine was as close to a racially ambiguous Disney princess as I was going to get. That should 100 percent be read as a burn on how Disney's animated Jasmine reads less as Middle Eastern and more as "white girl with a tan at Coachella," at least visually. She wears a crop top and a bejeweled headband and has a pet tiger. You can probably see her popping Molly in the background of a scene if you watch closely.

Mulan, however, was definitively Chinese. She was unabashedly Asian. Twelve-year-old me took her Asianness extremely bashedly. Twelve-year-old me had already spent years being referred to as Chinese by both peers and adults with an unmistakable tone of name-calling. Asian and Chinese were one and the same to much of the very white suburban town where I grew up. Likewise, "Asian" was synonymous with "foreign" or "different in a bad way" or "ugly" or "if you wear your hair in a bun someone will definitely call you a sumo wrestler or a geisha because who can tell you all apart anyway?!?!?" The Venn diagram of people who can name thirteen different dog breeds but think all Asians look the same is just a circle.

But Jasmine! Jasmine was definitively pretty! Jasmine was kind of exotic! Jasmine was different in a hot way! She was brown but in a white way! Middle school me had found her white-adjacent savior. And now, I had Jasmine's autograph. I was old enough to know this wasn't Jasmine's *actual autograph* but young enough to still feel like I had a tangible connection to a fictional character.

The week we spent at Disney World was hot and humid and very Florida. It was also summer, and I was also almost thirteen. With these circumstances combined, I chose to wear a bikini I bought off a clearance rack underneath a white ribbed boy's tank top I bought in a pack of six. It was my pubescent female horniness channeled into a single outfit. The bikini was red and patterned with big, white, tropical flowers. It was one of those cheap and terrible bikinis with the plastic loops connecting the straps to the triangle top, a feature that was both uncomfortable and not functional. I remember getting it and thinking, "This is what being sexy is."

At some point between water rides and Florida humidity and seeing a much older teen walking around in shorts and a bikini top, I took my tank top off. "I'm hot," I probably told my parents. *I'm hot*, I most definitely thought to myself. We continued walking around the Magic Kingdom, and I pretended not to frantically check if my areolas were showing every two minutes.

Despite the fact that I was actively frowning in every picture my dad took (being twelve is fun!!!), we all stood in line to get a picture with Baloo from *The Jungle Book*. We were next in line when a staff member walked up to me. My personal brand of delusion is the combination of thoughts I had when this happened:

I am either in very, very, extremely bad trouble, or they are about to ask me to be the next Jasmine. The staff member, a college-age woman, gently said I needed to put my shirt back on because they didn't want the characters posing in any picture that could be read as "suggestive." I was twelve. There is nothing so definitively female and pubescent as desperately wanting to be seen as sexual while simultaneously being humiliated by your own sexuality.

My seven-year-old sister, Ana, who was years away from knowing what puberty was let alone going through it, asked earnestly, "Do I have to put my shirt on, too?" She had also taken off her shirt earlier, likely because she saw me remove mine, and had been bopping around in a Limited Too tankini that covered the entirety of her torso. Everyone laughed. I put my shirt back on.

I remember doing lots of very Disney things afterward. We did the tea cups. We saw the line to see Mickey (none of us cared enough to wait in it). My dad, the self-designated photographer of the trip, took pictures of us eating giant turkey legs and standing with the Epcot ball in the background and being hot and flushed and dehydrated. For being the happiest place on earth, Disney is packed to the brim with screaming children, crying toddlers, begrudging teenagers, kids barfing, adults barfing, parents complaining about the cost of lemonade, children complaining about not getting the particular plastic trinket that they want, and very forced smiles.

After sufficiently shitting ourselves at the Haunted Mansion, we walked toward Aladdin's magic carpet ride. I stood in line with my mom and Ana while my dad and brothers quickly split another turkey leg or something. If you aren't familiar, the mechanics of the magic carpet ride are pretty straightforward: you pick a carpet like you would an animal on a carousel; the ride goes around in a circle, rotating around a giant pole, while you control how high or low your carpet flies using a lever in front of you. Magic is nowhere when you are twelve and someone just told you to put your shirt back on.

My mom and sister rode together in the carpet ahead of me. I rode alone, likely by angst-driven choice. However, even in my preteen angst, I was a sucker for an amusement park ride. I remember being at least a little excited to pick a carpet and loudly hum "A Whole New World" to myself. I remember allowing myself to stop stifling a smile and making the carpet go up as high as the lever would allow. I remember Ana turning around and waving and feeling more happiness than embarrassment. I remember the moment, about midway through the ride, when I caught a whiff of something bad and looked down at my feet to see that I had picked the carpet with an actual human shit in it.

My dad captured the moment shortly after this realization. It is a perfectly framed picture. My mom and Ana are in the foreground, smiling together in a gleeful embrace. I am in the background, riding in my magic carpet alone, with the kind of aggressively indifferent expression you can only make when you are twelve and just realized you are riding the magic carpet someone shit in.

I let the carpet mechanically float back down, trying not to let anything other than my butt and feet touch the ride. I got off the ride and met up with my mom and sister who were windswept with whimsy and also actual wind. They asked me what was wrong as my grimace was more grimace-y than usual. "My magic carpet had poop in it," I said. I bet Jasmine never had to put up with that shit.

A TIME LINE OF
MY ONLINE PERSONAS

2002: SprGrl919@hotmail.com

This ancient MSN-adjacent relic was my very first email address. I intended for "SprGrl" to stand for "Supergirl," though it just as easily could have meant "Spear Girl" or "Spider-Girl" or "Spare Grill." I had seen approximately zero Superman movies and wasn't particularly interested in superheroes at the time or currently. However, *The Princess Diaries* soundtrack featured a song with the lyrics "I'm Supergirl / And I'm here to save the world / And I wanna know / Who's gonna save me?" I also had exactly one shirt from Kohl's with the Superman logo on it. So, when pressed to think of an email address, I was like, "Hmmm, yeah, that could work." The "919" comes from my childhood address because I didn't understand the concept of not revealing too much information to strangers.

The only people who knew that email address were my parents, with whom I lived and had no reason to email ever, and a handful of friends at school. My email correspondence with those friends, whose email addresses started with things like "snowgurl" and "sk8rchick," was composed primarily of quotes we found on strangers' LiveJournals, like "fLiRtInG iS mY AnTi-DrUg" and low-res gifs from FunnyJunk.com. We also sent each other a lot of Dollz.

If you had a dial-up connection and went to middle school in the early '00s, you probably remember Dollz. Describing Dollz as merely digital Barbie dolls does them a disservice. Dollz were like if a Bratz doll and a paper doll met behind a dumpster after school and the Bratz doll was like, "Okay, I found out what 'BJ' stands for." They were tiny, pixelated hot girls with simple looping graphics of twinkling stars or a marquee above their head blinking SHOPAHOLIC. On websites like Dollz Mania, you could create your own Doll, picking which pink mesh messenger cap and flared white pants went best together (none of them). You could also select from hundreds of premade Dollz, all with twelve-inch waists, perfectly round boobs, and thighs that had never and would never meet.

My female friends and I would spend our nights making collections of Dollz we thought looked like us as Charlie's Angels, us in a girl band, us but goth, or, most often, us in our imagination. "I would totally wear those low-rise jeans and black, cropped halter top," I'd think while picking popcorn out of my braces and wiping it on my Target clearance-rack shirt. The only objective in playing with Dollz was to make the hottest one and send it to your friends. There was no compliment quite like someone greeting you in first period, handing you a full piece of paper with one, nearly microscopic, fifty-pixel Doll printed on it, and saying, "I thought this looked like you."

If my taste in Dollz was any indication, I believed hot girls had voluminous hair that was wider than their waist, eyes that took up 75 percent of their face, and the suggestion of a nose rather than a nose itself. None of the Dollz ever looked straight-on; they always had their head slightly turned because even digital women have a "good side."

One day, in seventh grade, my friend Alyssa printed off an email chain between me, her, and our friend Sami. This was a normal occurrence as we'd spend free periods cutting out the Dollz we made the night before and taping them to our assignment notebooks, adorning one of our few pieces of property with these tiny digital girls. All was fine and good until a cool boy got ahold of the printed-off emails during indoor recess. I'll call him Taylor because that was his name.

After paging through the printed emails of Dollz, Taylor laughed and asked, "Who's 'Sperm Girl'?" The other boys with names like Spencer or Brandon started laughing, too. At first, Alyssa, Sami, and I didn't get it. While decidedly slutty and intentionally sexual, none of our Dollz looked particularly sperm-y. So, he asked again. "Who's 'Sperm Girl 919'?"

He was talking about my email address. To boys who thought the word "sperm" was both a setup and a punch line, my vowelless allusion was lost on them. Also, it would have been equally embarrassing to correct them by saying, "It's supposed to mean 'Supergirl,' and you will address me as such."

The boys called me "Sperm Girl" for the next couple of weeks. Despite my begging, my dad wouldn't let me change my email address since I had just gotten that one. (Email addresses strangely felt like a finite resource in 2002.) I stayed "Sperm Girl

919" until high school, when I adopted an even more humiliating email address.

2003: GummiBGirl

In middle school, my classmates started using AOL Instant Messenger or, as we abbreviated it, AIM. I'm not sure how I convinced my parents to let me download the messaging program when they were cautious of me googling anything that could be remotely construed as salacious. (*What do you mean you need to look up 'Venus'? Is that code for something?!?*") But somehow I did and was left with yet another opportunity to absolutely own myself with a terribly named online persona.

The screen name I chose was "GummiBGirl." While there are a handful of ways to misinterpret that jumble of letters and what the "b" might stand for, I knew it couldn't be read as "sperm." This was really my only screen name stipulation.

The "b" stood for "bear" because "Gummi Bear Girl" was already taken. I enjoy gummi bears, but I wouldn't say they've ever been integral to who I am as a person either in real life or online. They're not even in my top three favorite candies. (It goes: Kit Kats, Peanut Butter M&Ms, Twix. Then there's a gap, and then Life Savers Gummies, and then there's another gap, and then it's *maybe* gummi bears.)

The formula for creating screen names in middle and high school was simple:

- Pick an animal, a dessert, a season, or a sport.

- Add the word "girl" or some variation of it (e.g., gurl, grl, girlie, chica, chick).

- Optional: add some numbers by smashing your face on the top row of the keyboard or typing whatever year you were born.

- Make sure the name doesn't unintentionally look like the word "sperm," "sex," "penis," "poop," or "vagina."

I remained GummiBGirl on AIM until I thought of something "better."

September 2004: ThInKiNpInK642

I eventually upgraded to the screen name I would have throughout all of high school: ThInKiNpInK642. It was random! It was obscure! It meant absolutely nothing at all! For those reasons, my teenage self thought, "Yes. That name is much better."

"642" are the numbers you'd press on a phone keypad to spell out "Mia." I'm sure I added them in hopes someone, anyone, would ask why I chose those particular numbers, but this is the first time I've ever explained it.

To dissect "Think in Pink," here's what you need to know. (1) I had a Pink Panther–themed pajama set that I loved. (2) This was shortly before "Check on It" by Beyoncé came out and was featured on the 2006 *Pink Panther* soundtrack, reaffirming my screen name choice. And that's all the background I have for you.

ThInKiNpInK642 saw me through a lot: my first boyfriend,* that boyfriend breaking up with me a couple of months later, hours of online flirting with upperclassmen who would never

---

* Here, "boyfriend" means "a guy who asked me out on AIM and would sometimes look at me in the hallway."

look at me in real life, and another boyfriend,* who I learned wanted to dump me after he changed his standard Away Message from "I LUV MIA" to "AMBER K. IS MY BEST FRIEND."

October 2004: seXxxiiGurL69

This was still during the Think in Pink era, and I'm not sure whether this is an exact screen name I used, but I definitely created accounts with something similar to it. This was my teenage equivalent to a burner phone. While playing online Pictionary or games like it, I'd be prompted to make up a username that would be displayed to other players. This was before I had Facebook, so I didn't have to worry about the name somehow linking to a social media account, exposing my horny alter ego. Depending on my mood and whether my parents had gone to bed, I'd type in a name my teenybopper brain believed conveyed some degree of sexual appeal.

The formula for creating horny screen names was simple:

- Pick a horny word (e.g., sexy, hot, baby) or some variation of it (e.g., sexi, hottie, babii).

- Add a Hot Girl name (e.g., Vicky, Victoria, Vickie) OR a variation of the word "girl" (e.g., gurl, grl, girlie, chica, chick).

- Optional: add Xs or 69 for good measure.

- Make sure the name doesn't unintentionally look like the word "sperm," "penis," "poop," or "vagina."

---

* Here, "boyfriend" means "a guy who asked me out on AIM and went to one (1) high school football game with me."

In the middle of a Pictionary round, I'd privately message the other members of my chat or, more often, wait until someone messaged me something clever and subtle like "a/s/l" (shorthand for "age/sex/location"). I'd lie and say "24/f/nyc" or "18/f/chicago." I was a fourteen-year-old girl in a Wisconsin suburb until I had the shield of the internet. Then I was a twentysomething college student in a major city with the same proportions as the Dollz I made online. Most of the time, the conversations were limited to normal small talk or commentary on the game we were playing. Occasionally, things would escalate.

They'd say something flirtatious like "i bet ur really hot," and I'd respond equally flirtatiously like, "i am." Sometimes they'd ask me to send a picture and I'd search "pretty girl blonde" and send along a pixelated Google image of whatever pretty, blonde, white stranger I felt like being that night.

There was only one time, in the entirety of my AIM life, I came close to having cybersex with someone. It was in the messages of one of these games. Things started off slowly, each of us asking the obligatory "a/s/l" and the other responding "nice." Then one of us asked the other what they were wearing, I don't remember who. The answer was probably "pajamas;)" to which the natural reply would have been "sounds sexy."

If you're familiar with phone sex or sexting, which I'm sure you are, you perv, you know how these conversations sometimes go. There's buildup. There's teasing. There's something said that could be read as provocative, left dangling in the conversation like a ripe peach. If/when the other person takes a bite, it's go time. That is not how this conversation went.

Shortly after "pajamas;)" one of us said, "Wanna cyber?" and the other said, "Sure." That was it. There was no flirting with double entendres or flirting in general. One person was like, "Should we do sex now?" and the other said, "Okay, yes, I know how to do that." Then there was silence.

"You go first," they said after a pause. To which I flirted back, "No, you go first." This continued for maybe a minute, with more long pauses in between. Then, without warning, they signed off.

I like to imagine that, on the other side of the screen, it was another fourteen-year-old girl in the suburban Midwest. I assume that she, like me, was many years away from anyone other than her family practitioner ever seeing her naked. I imagine this in part because any alternative would be gross and probably illegal. I also think, if she was anything like me, she would have understood the rush of embarrassment, excitement, fear, horniness, and shame I felt after I also signed off.

December 2004: PerfectAsImEverGonnaBe

This was the name of the first blog I had in high school. It still lives on the internet if you really want to go down a rabbit hole. However, there's only one entry because I either forgot my log-in information promptly after signing out the first time or I wanted to change the URL from "gonna" to "gunna," or maybe it was both.

In the annals of iconic first lines, among "Call me Ishmael" and "It was the best of times, it was the worst of times," there will be this, the first line from my first blog post: "So I've finally started one of these . . ."

The post goes on to include such poetic lines as "Jesse Mc-Cartney is dreamy:)" and such thoughtful self-reflections as "I say Like too much." It ends with this devastating line: "Ugh I love how just as I have to go I know what I want to write . . ." Much like my first and only post, this blog doesn't deserve much attention.

2005: Don't Rain on My P.a.R.a.D.e

This was the name of the second blog I had in high school. I don't remember if "Don't Rain on My Parade" was part of the URL or just the title at the top of the blog, but both are equally bad. My blog was essentially a public, online diary, where I talked about my day with the hyperbolic drama you'd expect of a high schooler. I used code names for boys I had crushes on. I complained about teachers having the absolute *nerve* to assign homework. I typed in bad fonts and lots of colors and employed the use of bold type often.

I remember my blog being well-read among my classmates, though I'm not sure if that was the actual case or just what I imagined to be true. I know on a few occasions, people at school would comment about one of my posts. There is nothing like the sweet awkwardness of someone looking you in your real-life eyes and saying, "I liked that thing you did on the internet." It was nice to feel good at something, being that I was a teen girl who simultaneously felt bad and perfect and too seen and completely invisible. It was nice to have an audience for the same reason.

Once, a boy anonymously confessed his love for me in the comments section of my blog. The idea of someone leaving me a secret love note was one of the reasons (subconscious or not) I started a blog in the first place. Unfortunately, nothing happened. I found out who it was and was disappointed that it was just a guy I did theater with and not, I don't know, Jesse McCartney, lurking on my blog.

In a fit of needing to start fresh, I deleted the whole blog after high school graduation. Sometimes I wish I had kept more remnants of my high school musings. Most times, I'm humiliated when I remember anything from that era of my life. All of the time, I am grateful that social media and YouTube didn't fully exist until I was out of high school. I would have been a total and complete menace.

2006: CiaoBella0906

This is the beginning of the email address that usurped "SprGrl919." (Sperm Girl is dead. Long live Sperm Girl.) I had this email throughout most of high school, until I started applying for colleges and internships. I eventually became aware enough to know that future employers would take one look at my email and go, "Yeah, no. We're not going to hire this Limited Too shirt that came to life."

When I still remembered the log-in information, I went through my old inbox to see if there was anything worth salvaging. (Read: love notes I'd forgotten about.) Though the inbox was mostly spam and email chain letters from distant aunts, the drafts folder was a nasty little gold mine.

One draft was an email I intended to send myself, the contents of which were for a school project. The email had no subject line and was completely blank save for a PowerPoint presentation on the Holocaust and my personalized email signature that read *HoLLa BaCk*. My fifteen-year-old self in a tacky, tacky nutshell.

What else did I think was worth saving in an email draft when I was in high school? Why, the AIM conversation in which my middle school boyfriend and I broke up, of course! Cool! Super healthy and good! Here is an excerpt from that conversation, a two-line play, if you will:

ME: how come u refuse to do anything with me?

HIM: cuz u cant handle not being able to see me

Most of my drafts were saved AIM conversations, angsty and confusingly sexual poems I found online, lyrics to songs I made up, lyrics to songs Nelly made up, and a lot of rAnDoM cApItaL-iZaTiOn.

Because I'm sure you were wondering, "0906" is my birthday, September 6. Mark it on your calendars. Send me gifts and lyrics to Nelly songs.

2008: Mia Mercado

I am among a generation of young adults whose relationship with internet privacy has changed completely. It started with parents and teachers screaming at us to never publish any remotely revealing personal information online and has evolved into those same parents and teachers adding us on Facebook. Recently, my dad endorsed me for "creative writing" on the LinkedIn profile I forget is still active. This is the same dad who was wary of giving our Wi-Fi password to any friends who came over to study in high school.

The idea of "cultivating a personal brand" online is so gross and strange, but it's what's expected. If you don't have social media accounts, you're either a creep, a recluse, or too famous to care. Even Oprah has Instagram. Oprah! If even Oprah can't ignore the pressure to present herself on the internet, how am I supposed to?

Maybe, one day, I'll figure out how to care less about Twitter. Maybe, eventually, I won't take it personally when a piece I write gets less Facebook attention than someone sharing a picture of a tree with the caption "Nature, am I right?" Who knows. Maybe I'll just rebrand as GummiBGirl.

YOU'RE FROM THE MIDWEST?!
WHAT'S THAT LIKE?

When people are surprised I'm from the Midwest, I take it as a compliment. In part because I know that's how they mean it. They're not called "fly-over states" because people really want to "fly over there to South Dakota, dontcha know." Though I'm sure Midwestern optimism would try to skew it that way. There are a lot of things about being born and raised and continuing to live in the Midwest as an adult that are strange and specific to the middle of the country. Things like how I personally knew the only other Asian family in my hometown. Like how my high school class could be divided into whose family was Catholic, whose was Lutheran, and the remainder would be maybe two kids. The fact that young people who aren't millionaires or related to Kardashians can buy a house.

I know the Midwest can seem cultureless or uncouth or so cheap and convenient it's suspicious, and you know what? Sometimes it's all of those things. But I don't think that's necessarily limited to any one part of the country. The cultureless and uncouth parts, at least. I'll pour one of my $2 beers out in honor of your coastal rent costs.

New York can smell like dumpster piss, and LA can feel like straightener-fried extensions, but we'll all still tune in to watch a group of mostly white friends navigate those big cities at 8/7 central. I'm starting to wonder if maybe we only culturally care about the things we do because we're told to and shown how. The Midwest can be overly polite, mayo-based, stupidly afford-able trash, and I'm starting to realize I love it.

If you're wondering what the Midwest is like, allow me to be your corn-fed, surprisingly only half-white tour guide.

Being from the Midwest is like being from anywhere else in the United States, just five to ten years in the past.

It's that feeling you get when you drive on a country road between two seemingly endless cornfields and are like, "Huh. Yeah, that's a lot of corn."

It's the loud, nasal whisper of someone saying, "Just gonna sneak by ya real quick" while scooching into a church pew.

Living in the Midwest is so cool. It's also warm, hot, icy, au-tumn, three feet of snow forever, no sun and then too much sun, three months of gray slush, the idea of springtime but never re-ally experiencing springtime, and apple picking.

It's seeing a cow and going, "Cow."

The Midwest is where horse girls go to become horsewomen.

It's wearing overalls to be trendy but ending up matching the farmer who is also shopping at this Farm & Fleet.

Have you ever seen Lake Michigan in the summertime, beautiful and vast, lined with three thousand dead alewife fish? That's the Midwest, baby.

In the Midwest, Facebook is just for telling you who from high school is married to each other. Every pop-up notification is like, "Wait, wasn't he a *senior* when she was a *freshman*?!"

Being from the Midwest is all about your mom dropping you and your friends off at the mall, which is twenty to forty-five minutes away from the suburb where you live. You'll call her when you guys are done? Oh, honey, she'll just be waiting in the parking lot with this new James Patterson novel. Make sure you put the directions into the GSP . . . er, GPS . . . er, whatever you kids call it. Oh, hang on to the grab handle, mama's gonna make a hard turn. Do you know which buildings around here used to be a Blockbuster? Don't worry, mom'll tell ya.

The Midwest is where everything is measured in how many hours away you are from your childhood home.

It's like two dead deer on the side of the road arguing over whether they like the Packers or the Bears.

It's like if every store you walked into was a Pottery Barn, and by that I mean it's extremely white.

It's like "wisCAAAHNsin" not "Wisconsin."

The Midwest is that feeling you get when you find free parking, but the free parking is literally everywhere, if that makes sense?

It's like seeing a celebrity at the grocery store, but instead of a celebrity, it's your local CBS weatherman or the girl who sat behind you in pre-algebra but moved in eighth grade.

It's never knowing if that person is smiling at you just to be friendly or because you babysat them in middle school.

It's having to write a thank-you card to your priest for coming to your birthday party even though you only agreed to invite him because you thought priests weren't allowed to eat cake.

The Midwest is where the world's supply of "ope" comes from.

Being from the Midwest is the best. And if you disagree, well . . . no one here will fight you on it. We're a nice people.

MAMMA MIA

Like the stereotype of the suburban Midwest I sometimes am, I used to think I'd be an elementary school teacher when I grew up. Everything around me had primed me to spend the rest of my days surrounded by kids between the ages of "baby" and "can't quite use an oven on their own." I had younger siblings and grew up around younger cousins. I attended, graduated from, and some might even say peaked in elementary school. I'd been babysitting since I was in—and I cannot emphasize this enough—fifth grade. In the same way you likely don't remember your first step or trying solid food for the first time, I don't remember when I first changed a diaper. I assumed this was a normal part of growing up until, as an adult, I saw many of the childless men around me panic in the presence of a baby.

I loved babysitting. I still love it. It's always felt easy to make kids like me, something that's often felt forced with my peers. At ten and eleven, I was better at being A Little Grown-up than A Child Who Acts Her Age. Perhaps it was my enrollment in the accelerated reading program or the fact that I grew facial hair long before the boys in my class, but parents trusted me (a child) with their own children.

This is something I've only thought of as strange in my late twenties. Have you seen a middle schooler recently? Did you know that seventh graders are a literal twelve years old? Do you remember being twelve? Being so horny your brain and butt might explode while also being terrified of your own body? Having homework, your main if not only responsibility, cause you to have full-on, nightly emotional breakdowns because *there's just, like, A LOT going on right now that you don't know about, MOM!* Imagine handing your baby to that, leaving for a couple of hours, and returning to pay them in cash.

I saved a lot of the money I made from babysitting. My family was the exact combination of financially stable and money conscious (also see: half-Asian) that the balance of saving and avoiding unnecessary spending has been instilled in me since birth. I still always order the cheapest burger on the menu, like my dad will find out if I don't.

I didn't start babysitting because I needed money or because my parents pressured me into getting a job. I did it because I genuinely enjoyed being around kids younger than me. I liked having some semblance of authority. I liked having adults praise me for something that came naturally to me. I liked how the kids I watched made me feel cool and smart and good at playing pop covers on the guitar. Babysitting made me feel how I assume a straight white dude feels every day.

I also liked having stories to tell my friends, anecdotes that provided an excuse for me to tell Drew C. all about my day in hopes that he'd be wooed by my natural maternal instinct at fifteen. I spent most of my summers in high school babysitting. I'd watch kids during the day, making sure they stayed alive while I looked for the parents' stash of Diet Coke in the basement fridge or tried to figure out where they kept their kids' old Halloween candy. At night, I'd hang out with my friends and regale them with my tales of babysitting. "The kids were insane today," I'd say, like a weathered mom of four.

I told them about the kid who crocodile-death-rolled while I was trying to change his diaper, how he smeared his own shit on the carpet, an air mattress, and the walls in three different rooms. Have you ever tried to get poop out of popcorn walls? Would not recommend.

I talked about the kid who greeted me in a full WWII uniform after I came out of the bathroom. He'd been wearing a t-shirt and shorts when I went to go pee not five minutes before. "This was my grandpa's," he said, and I had to be like, "Extremely cool, Bobby, but can we maybe put that knife down?"

Then there was the four-year-old girl who wouldn't stop scream-crying in the bathroom, begging me to call her dad. When I asked what was wrong, she sobbed, "My poop! Is too! BIG!" She wasn't constipated. She had just done one very big poop, and it scared her.

In between going to town on a bunch of pumpkin-shaped Reese's in April, snooping through bedside tables and medicine cabinets, and eating oatmeal creme pies while I made myself boxes of mac and cheese, I was a bomb-ass babysitter. I'd do crafts with the kids, in part because that sounded like a cute *Baby-Sitters Club*-esque thing to do. I taught them songs on the piano despite how tone-deaf and uninterested they were. I took them to parks and pools and wherever else was within walking distance. I also made a neighbor kid named Greg piss his pants a little because I startled him while playing Cops and Robbers. This isn't an example of good babysitting, but it does show my comedic sensibility.

I never gave much thought to the parents whose kids I was watching. Only now am I fazed by the number of times I was driven home by dads who, in hindsight, were probably too tipsy to be operating a motor vehicle. Only now do I think about how weird it is that I babysat for my high school teachers. How they'd come home from happy hour, asking questions like, "Do you think I look older than Mr. Davis?" How I'd lie and pretend like anyone over twenty-two didn't look like a dinosaur to me.

The kids I used to babysit regularly are now years older than I was when I started watching them. They're posting thirst traps on Instagram and sharing questionable statuses on Facebook, and it makes me want to be like, "I used to have to start your apple for you, Dennis." I can't even imagine what parents must feel.

Like many girls who grew up in the Midwestern suburbs, primed by babysitting and Sunday school, I thought I'd start having kids by twenty-five "at the *latest*." I remember being in elementary school, calculating at what age I'd need to start having kids in order to be young and hot when my hypothetical children started going to school, learning to drive, going to college, and eventually repeating the cycle themselves. "I don't want to be a super old grandma," I'd think well before having my first period.

I'm turning thirty soon, and sometimes I worry that my body has a broken clock, forgetting to chime "baby" every hour. It's strange, after spending so much of your life terrified you'll get pregnant, to suddenly reach a point where you begin worrying you may not be able to grow a child inside you even if you tried. To have relatives, teachers, and congresspeople scream "ABSTI-NENCE" at your vacant belly and then pivot, seemingly over-night, to scream "BABY." To have distant family members and government agencies look at your body as a host for life instead of life itself. To have your gender function as a living résumé whose job options begin and end at "mother."

It seems like kismet or a curse that "mamma" comes before my name so easily. My grandma lovingly calls me "Mamma Mia." (Thanks, ABBA.) I have always felt like a mother bird, and only now am I wondering whether that is in my nature or nurture or both at the same time.

I have yet to have "baby fever" as an adult. My body has re-mained at a steady 98.6 degrees Fahrenheit, selfishly childless. My symptoms are more tied to sweating at the idea of "needing" to have a baby "soon." If I'm being honest, the most appealing part of being pregnant right now is that I'd actually have an ex-cuse for wanting to nap and eat away most of the day. My ten-year IUD will expire when I turn thirty-five, the same age that preg-nancies are scientifically dubbed "geriatric." I wonder if I will be ready for kids by then. As if anyone feels ready ever.

I worry a lot about being pregnant, what my body will and won't do. I worry what my post-pregnant brain will and won't think. I worry whether or not to circumcise the son I may or may not have. I worry about how I'll talk to my daughter about any-thing at all. Am I doomed to have some sort of post-birth Fran-kenpussy? Will I get a parallel C-section scar to match the one that currently stretches across my stomach?

I was born with an ileal stricture, a piece of tissue blocking my small intestine. This is a scientific way to say that I could not shit when I was a baby. Pooping, as you may know, is a key part of being a baby. I used to use it as my Fun Fact on first-day introductions. "When I was a baby, I almost died because I couldn't poop," I'd announced to my fellow fourth graders. "Oh. Well. We're glad you didn't die," the teacher would respond, unblinkingly.

My parents still talk about how scary it was, their ten-day-old child vomiting up gunk that didn't look like the right kind of gunk babies usually vomit. The idea of doctors operating on a ten-day-old baby didn't fully faze me until I held my newborn niece for the first time. Babies, if you can believe it, are tiny. They are soft little noodles with heads too heavy for their weak baby neck muscles to lift. The fact that there are people smart enough to diagnose something hidden in a baby's intestines, and that there are medical instruments delicate enough to fix a baby's insides, is all horrifying and incredible and just generally bonkers. I still don't understand how they haven't made indestructible phone cases but for babies.

This isn't to say I don't trust myself with a child. I know I am great at holding children—part of which comes from the confidence of someone who has always been expected to know how to hold a child. I have friends whose husband's first time changing a diaper came with their first child, friends (male) with pregnant partners who ask if they want to hold a baby "for practice." The idea of never having held a baby seems like a cardinal sin to me, though not one ever preached aloud in the Catholic Church.

People applaud, cheer, swoon over what a great father my husband, Riley, will make every time he does something as brave as standing next to a baby. Riley will* be a wonderful parent. He is patient and smart and has worked as an elementary or middle school teacher his entire adult life. He's better trained to be around kids than most of our peers with children of their own. Still, my potential parenthood is expected, where his is lauded. We each have our roles, though his is always "Man" and mine is "Childless Wife."

Riley's biological clock ticks in sync with mine. Every time after we babysit our nieces or hang out with our friends who have kids, we look at each other and perform a ten-second play called *Should We Have Kids?* It goes like this:

"Not yet, right?"

"Right."

"So cute though."

"Yes, the cutest!"

"And great for them."

"Yes, we love it for them."

". . . But not yet for us."

"Oh my god, not yet."

---

* I just went back and forth between "will" and "would." Even hypothetical me is nervous about having kids.

DEPRESSION ISN'T A COMPETITION, BUT, LIKE, WHY AREN'T I WINNING?

I think a lot about this 2005 commercial for the antidepressant Cymbalta that's all about how "depression hurts." We open on a Sad Woman.* She's lying on a couch, blanket askew, face lit by the television. A classic depression scene. A moody female voiceover asks where depression hurts. The Sad Woman is still on the couch. *Everywhere*, the same voiceover responds breathily. We see a montage of disappointed children, a dog waiting to play fetch, a woman walking away from her husband at the dinner table. The voiceover asks who depression hurts. We see a person sighing while looking into the middle distance. *Everyone*, she exhales, exhausted that she is the only one participating in this question-and-answer exercise. I don't remember how the

---

* Actor portrayal, of course. Wouldn't want to see an actual depressed person. Yuck.

commercial ends but certainly not with me calling my doctor to order "one Cymbalta to go, please."

But I'll admit, the voiceover does sound similar to the way my depressed brain talks to itself.

Should we get out of bed yet?

*No. *deep sigh**

But it's already noon.

*Okay. *even deeper sigh**

And it's a weekday.

*Correct. *yet another sigh**

Is this me being lazy or depressed?

*Yes. *sighs while looking knowingly toward camera**

Most of my experience with depression has involved asking myself and the people closest to me whether I am "sad enough" to be clinically depressed. Am I depressed in the normal "ha ha aren't we all so sad right now" way, or am I, like, *depressed* depressed?

If I have depression, am I supposed to cry a lot, all the time? Should I not be crying ever? Should everything around me make me feel bad? Should I not feel anything at all? How long do I have to stay in bed in the morning? How late do I need to stay up at night? Can I technically be depressed if I still laugh at the episode of *Bob's Burgers* where Louise has a crush on a member of a boy band and that attraction manifests itself in her wanting to slap the boy in the face? What if it's the fourth time I've watched the episode that day? What has to happen to my appetite? If I go to McDonald's twice in a week, does that count as a cry for help? If I tweet about eating McDonald's being a cry for help, does that make me depressed or relatable? Would being more relatable on Twitter cure my depression altogether?

I was officially diagnosed with depression at the beginning of 2018. In hindsight, that was far from when I'd first started feeling depressed. I'd seen a counselor a couple of years prior, at the beginning of 2016. She thought I might have premenstrual dysphoric disorder, which is like PMS on X Games mode. After reading the common symptoms (extreme mood shifts, sadness, irritability), the counselor said, "Hmm. Maybe everyone with a period has this." If you're wondering whether that's a reassuring thing to hear from a medical professional, the answer is I stopped going to her pretty soon after that session.

Before that, I thought my depression came and went with the birth control pill I started taking in 2013 and stopped in 2015. Before that still, I thought I'd rid myself of any deep spells of sadness after graduating from college in 2011. (Most of what I remember of college is me, living at home, and crying a lot in my twin-size bed.) I'd diagnose myself with Bad Relationships, Lack of Friends, Watching Too Much *Law & Order: SVU*. Anything to avoid admitting that maybe the depression call was coming from inside the house. *Everyone gets sad*, I'd think. *It's normal to feel sad*, I'd say. *It's healthy, even*, I'd justify before settling into my daily three-hour afternoon "nap."

I don't remember my family having many in-depth discussions about mental health growing up. I know my mom, who experiences chronic illness and physical pain, slept a lot during the day and was up at strange times during the night. I know my dad said nothing when my mom would wordlessly leave the house, angry-crying or sad-crying or both. She'd leave alone, take the car, come back in a few hours, and neither of my parents said anything when she returned. I also remember my mom allotting us an unlimited number of "mental health" days from school. If I was sad, she'd pick me up at the front office, say I had an orthodontist appointment despite having gotten my braces off years ago, and let me sleep in her bed for the afternoon. Such are the pros and cons of having a parent who understands this particular brand of sadness.

Ana and I play this one depression game a lot. The game goes like this: We say how we can't be *that* depressed because we got out of bed to pee. We say we can't be *that* sad because we went "aww" at a dog once. We say we can't be *that* sick because, well, we're still here and alive, aren't we?

One of the questions counselors or therapists or general practitioners ask when you say the magic word "depressed" is whether you recognize any patterns in what brings on your depressive episodes. Before I got on medication, long before I admitted to myself and those around me that I have depression, I only had these mismatched scenes of sadness committed to memory.

I remember downing gin and tonics at a townie bar while home for Christmas one year. I remember catching up with friends, mentioning that maybe my birth control was making me depressed. I remember laughing afterward and hoping I said it all in a joking enough way. Later, we all went to this McMansion where my friend was house-sitting. I drunkenly snuck into a basement storage closet with shelves and shelves of these amber glass apothecary bottles. *Where does depression hurt?* my voiceover asked. There were so many bottles. They were pretty and tiny and all my drunken brain could think about was how much I wanted one. There had to be at least fifty of these bottles. There's no way anyone would notice if I took one, I justified. I grabbed one and carried it around like a trophy all night. *Everywhere*, I answered. The bottle has been to two states, through two moves, and lived in two different homes with me. It still sits on my bedside dresser.

I remember, a year or so later, being at a restaurant called Houlihan's with my boyfriend at the time. I left him to wait for our table in the lobby while I went to a bathroom stall to sob. If you've never been to a Houlihan's, it's a great place to have a depressive breakdown. It's similar to a Macaroni Grill or even a Cheesecake Factory in that it's hard to pin down just how fancy or casual it is. You could see a group of high schoolers in glittery lamé, picking at Caesar salads before the homecoming dance seated next to a two-top with a person dining alone, unshowered and wearing sweats, and none of it would seem out of place. I don't remember what I was sad about, why my body insisted on letting out a few silent sobs in a public bathroom. I don't remember if anyone saw me wiping snot on my sleeve as I walked out of the bathroom. I don't remember if my ex asked what was wrong when I returned to the table. I do remember that the macaroni and cheese had pot roast in it, and it was delicious. I think about it more than I do my ex.

I remember the time I came back to my apartment after having a shitty time at a wedding. They played that "angel is the centerfold" song during the reception. That wasn't the only reason I had a shitty time, but it's the one that sums it up the best. When I got home, the guy I was seeing was in the living room, sipping whiskey and working on a screenplay. I was upset. He wanted to keep writing. We didn't talk. I'd never been so angry to be part of some pseudo-Zach-Braff-directed indie movie in my life. Where was this scene in the Cymbalta montage?

I remember, later that year, getting ready to go to a costume party for an acquaintance's birthday and all of a sudden panicking that I looked too stupid to go out in public. I remember standing in the living room, half-crying, half-hyperventilating, fully freaking out, and telling this to the guy I was with. *Who does depression hurt?* the voiceover asks breathlessly. The way he looked at me—with a combination of disgust, exhaustion, embarrassment, and confusion—is something I will remember forever. *Everyone*, I whisper.

In January of 2018, I started the generic version of Lexapro, my current antidepressant weapon of choice. Because no one told me what the process of getting on an antidepressant would look like, I will impart my specific journey unto you.

Step 1: Feel fine most of the time.

"Fine" may be feeling sad or neutral or nothing or intense happiness in regular-ish cycles. If you were to chart your feelings, they would look like teen acne: bumpy but in a way that you assume comes with the territory of being a person.

Step 2: Have a Bad Day.

You'll say these sync up with your period starting or your period stopping or the week before your period starts or the third day of your cycle or the week-and-a-half after your cycle ends. *I'm just feeling emotional*, you might say. *This is just a momentary low*, you'll lie. The Bad Day will usually happen at night.

Step 3: Repeat Steps 1 and 2 again and again and again.

Sometimes a Step 1.5 will come into play where you think, *See? The Bad Day ended and now I'm fine. Everything is fine!!!* The following Step 2 will hit you swiftly. Vengefully, even.

Step 4: Have the first of many Conversations.

My recurring Conversation was with Riley, my then-fiancé, now husband. Riley is a golden retriever of a human being who somehow manifests his self-worth from—and I cannot stress this enough—himself. Once I said, "You know how you have days where you just don't like yourself." And he said, ". . . No?" We have very different experiences with mental health. Thus, our Conversation usually went something like this:

RILEY: Do you think you maybe need to talk to someone?

ME: I don't know.

RILEY: I think you need to talk to someone.

ME: I don't even know how I would start doing that.

RILEY: We can figure it out.

ME: I'm tired. And the idea of talking to someone makes me even more tired. And, *obviously*, I've thought about talking to someone. I, too, have seen an after-school special once. Allow me to verbally T-shirt-cannon all the reasons why talk therapy may not work and why going on medication is terrifying and how I know all the reasons I'm broken thus making me both perfect and unfixable. I just need to be upset for the next five minutes or ten hours or thirty years, and then I'll be fine.

Saying "I don't know" or "I don't care" were my shorthand for "I can't even begin to start thinking about this. I don't want to think. I don't want to make decisions right now, and anything you suggest will be something I've already thought about. Nothing you say can fix this, but, for the love of God, do not stop talking with me." Eventually, we'd get me back to Step 1.

Step 5: Continue repeating Steps 1 and 2.

Long swaths of time will pass. Sometimes you will have weeks and weeks without a Bad Day. Sometimes your days will be bad with a lowercase "b" and you'll think, *Everyone has bad days. It's fine to feel bad. Healthy, even.* Then, you'll have One Big Bad Day. Or maybe it will just feel Big because you'd convinced yourself you were fine. Or maybe this one will feel less Big than previous Bads, despite it being equally large and ferocious. *This low is fine,* you'll justify. *I've felt lower than this,* you'll say, pretending to remember a moment other than the one you're currently experiencing.

In the swirling of Bad and Low, it's hard not to feel resentful of Riley. (And then, if you're playing along at home, feel even worse for feeling resentful, and so on and so forth. Big Sadness, no Whammies!) How dare he be mentally stable. How absolutely cruel of him to have never been depressed. How heartless to try to help me through something I pray he will never experience firsthand.

Step X: Actually do something.

This step isn't assigned a number as these things don't tend to follow any real chronology. Much to Riley's dismay, my depression doesn't progress along any sort of actual time line. It doesn't come with any sort of manual or follow a framework that says, "If 'depressed,' simply say X and do Y. Then, voilà! No more depression."

During one particularly Low and Bad Day, I let Riley help me find a doctor. It was late. We were both crying in bed. He got out the laptop and googled something groundbreaking like "general practitioners near me." He showed me a doctor close by, covered by the insurance I'd bought through the marketplace. (Thanks, Obama.) I decided she looked enough like a doctor. So, Riley set up the appointment for me the next month. "Something about how I'm interested in starting antidepressants," I dictated as Riley typed the reason for my visit. I probably said it sarcastically (saying "interested" and "antidepressants" in the same sentence should automatically revoke my depression card), but Riley typed it with sincerity.

Telling a stranger, even one who is a doctor of medicine, that you are depressed is buck fucking wild. If you get uncomfortable having a new doctor take your measurements or look up your nose, imagine being asked questions like "Do you feel like you are a failure or that you have let yourself or your family down?" And then, imagine having to say yes!

After asking whether I'd had thoughts of wanting to hurt myself or others ("Not really," I said—a half-truth), my doctor told me a story about a former colleague whose child died from suicide years ago. Later, after telling her I'm half-Asian (a full truth and not part of the depression screening questions), she told me about another colleague who was Filipino and always invited her to karaoke. "Filipinos love their karaoke," she said before asking if I had a preferred pharmacy to pick up my prescription. I'd literally just finished telling her how I hate myself to a diagnosable degree, but yeah, sure, Dr. Saunders, let's talk about karaoke.

Getting medical confirmation that you are, in fact, depressed is both a gift and a curse. Congratulations! You're right! You DO have depression! Welcome to hell.

Starting antidepressants and getting back into regularly seeing a counselor hasn't solved my depression altogether, but knowing I'm doing something feels good. I still have Bad Days, but they aren't as frequent. I can actually count the number I've had in the past year on just a few fingers. I still don't like myself all the time. (Wow, can you believe it: you can't just take a pill that makes you like yourself.) I'm working on that, or at least I'm working on working on it. I don't feel like I'm waiting for an inevitable Bad Day, like I'm due for a scheduled breakdown because I've been feeling suspiciously okay. When I do have Bad Days, at least they have a ground floor instead of the way they used to feel like I could spiral downward forever into a dense nothingness.

That Cymbalta commercial has stuck with me in part because of how long I denied my own depression. *I can't be depressed*, I'd think, *because that would mean I'm literally hurting everyone around me*.

Perhaps the most terrible way to pull someone out of a depressive episode is to tell them their depression and self-hatred are hurting not only themselves but everyone around them. (This is second only to telling a cute anecdote about suicide and adding a racial microaggression for good measure.) I'd love to see an erectile dysfunction ad that shows a montage of people alone at a dinner table, a dog waiting to play fetch, children with their heads in their hands. Who does ED hurt? *Everyone.*

It's strange to have depression but not actively feel depressed. It feels like a lie to feel good, like other people will think I was faking it all. I think I thought an antidepressant would feel like a Band-Aid or an EpiPen. It'd stop the bleeding at the source, counter my allergic reaction to being alive. Honestly, it's more like a Claritin or some other over-the-counter allergy pill. If I take it regularly, my body won't sneeze sadness quite as much or with as gross a mucus.

While not doctor prescribed, there are some things that hit me in just the right happiness spot and create a shift in my depressive universe. I can feel a fog lift or a weight lessen, and suddenly I get why people feel happy sometimes. Here is a truncated list of some of the actual things that have helped pull me out of depressive spells:

- Jonas Brothers' 2019 Billboard Music Awards performance

- The warm sunny spot on my back deck

- Watching a tiny girl in a school uniform hoist herself up on a coffee shop counter to get a cup (I still tear up thinking about this)

- Going to Trader Joe's and buying expensive cheese I eat so quickly it should be illegal

- Remembering I love black olives, buying black olives, and eating a whole can of black olives

- My dog, Ava, being so small and stinky

- Ana waiting, crying, laughing with me until the Low and Bad leaves

- Riley being adamant that he will always want to stay

Sometimes I get so mad that there are people who wake up regularly feeling fine. That I have to take a pill that makes my brain not hate its host. That that pill fucks with my sleep as much as my actual depression does. That I've started taking nightly doses of melatonin or Target-brand ZzzQuil to get tired at a normal time. That that helps me fall asleep but makes me extra groggy in the morning. That my regular habit of sleeping in and feeling tired adds to feeling unproductive and that the feeling of unproductivity makes me hate myself more. That I can't just take a bath, sip on some Sleepytime tea, fall asleep easily, and wake up like, "Ahh, blessed morning to you and me."

Sometimes I'm fine. Such are the pros and cons of having depression. Not to sound like a Cymbalta commercial, but I've learned there isn't just one way to look, act, or be depressed. It took me a long time to get here, and I am, admittedly, still learning. I'd be lying if I said I don't still loop back to wondering whether I'm sad enough, happy enough, *enough* enough. Depression looks like everything and nothing, everyone and no one, all of it, all at once, none of the time.

I recently asked Ana where she thought my mom went when she'd leave the house. I'd assumed an empty parking lot. Ana thought she drove to a park near Lake Michigan. For the first time, instead of wondering, I asked my mom where she'd go when she'd leave.

"Can I be honest with you?" she said. "I don't remember doing that." This is one of the strange parts of growing to see your parents as whole, entire people. I'd guess my mom would say the same about learning your child is a whole, entire adult.

My mom talked to me about forgetting, about remembering, about whether there is a "normal" amount to feel sad, about her pain not being believed. My mom and I have different languages for our sadness. We map our emotional roads differently, though they both loop repeatedly around exhaustion and occasional hopelessness.

It'd be naive to say the way I process my depression isn't in some part influenced by the way my parents think about their own brains, their own bodies, their whole entire selves. I also know there are some stories that are not mine to tell. I often wonder whether the parts of myself I identify as "very much my mom" are me mimicking movements I've seen my mother perform or my body doing a dance it was always going to do. It's hard to look at yourself objectively, to not assign meaning or blame or quantify what is "good" or "bad" or "right" or "wrong."

"I accept myself for all the negatives," my mom wrote me once. I do, too, I think. At least, I'm trying to.

I recently rewatched that Cymbalta commercial. It's as melodramatic as I remember, but now it seems more funny than it does sad. Maybe that's all I can ask of everything, that it's more funny than sad. That life can be a little bit of everything all at the same time.

Part 2

ON BEING

Professional

These are stories on work, on school, on all things career-oriented. They are about the rituals we adopt when establishing our work routines, the things we make a habit of without really thinking twice about. (Drinking hot bean juice in the morning; staring at one screen during the day for work and another screen at night for fun; owning "dress pants" at all.)

Being female-presenting in the workplace is another onslaught of strangeness. It's unspoken rules about which men are going to hit on you and how you just need to expect that. It's the simultaneous, deep-seated fear that no one will flirt with you at this, your place of work, making you feel the truly fucked-up feeling of "Am I . . . not pretty enough to be harassed?" Then, as you're feeling shitty for feeling that feeling, some guy in middle management who graduated college three decades before you even had your first period is like, "I wish you were around when I was your age," winks at you, and the whole cycle repeats itself.

I've held jobs that, in their description, are objectively strange: greeting card editor, Instagram caption writer for a candy bar, author of this book. But if you think about it, no job makes sense. A team of people designed a Snuggie, and they got money for doing that. That's a job!

HOW TO QUIT YOUR JOB
AND CHANGE YOUR LIFE

My summer of 2016 lasted, roughly, three million lifetimes. Not only were we all deep in the throes of the presidential election, living blissfully unaware of our post–November 8 fate, but I was deeply entrenched in trying to figure out my professional life. Does the outcome of that presidential election have greater long-term cultural significance than me, a singular person, wondering, *but what should I do, like, job-wise?!?!?* I mean, sure. Is one of the most monumental political events of modern-day history perhaps worth more than a couple of throwaway contextual lines? Yeah, yeah, but I am what's important here. So, join me, won't you, as I make this all about me.

I began the summer by quitting a job where I'd just celebrated my five-year work anniversary. I'd never had to quit a job before. Every other job I had prior to that either had a specific end date (like internships and college work-study programs) or was short-term babysitting. You don't really quit babysitting. Either the kids eventually get old enough to make mac and cheese themselves or one day you just send a text like, "Sorry, Cathy, I'm not free to babysit next weekend because I actually moved to a different state! Give your monster of a six-year-old my regards!"

The decision to leave that job—my first Real Adult Job, which I'd started immediately after graduating from college—wasn't really a difficult one. The job itself was fine and paid well. For me, it was, at least initially, a literal dream job. I was the humor editor at a greeting card company. (Yes, it's the greeting card company you're thinking of.) My job, at its most basic level, was to decide which writers' jokes were funny enough to be on greeting cards. I was getting paid real, human money to pick a fart joke that was "most appropriate for a Father's Day card." (Insider tip: all fart jokes, large and small, wet and dry, are appropriate for a Father's Day card.)

If you've ever wondered who makes those greeting cards you immediately recycle after you take out your grandma's yearly birthday check, the answer is me. Well, me along with a team of editorial directors, art directors, writers, designers, production artists, marketing people, and business people, and that doesn't even begin to name the people involved in the process of actually printing and producing a card. There's a wild number of people who touch a greeting card before Granny seals it up with the dollar equivalent of however old you're turning. It's very "We Are the World" but with all our grubby hands encircling your birthday card.

My career as a greeting card editor started with the more serious, sentimental cards for holidays like Christmas and Mother's Day. I'd spend the hours between nine and five rewriting cards to say "I'm so grateful for you, Grandma" or "Being your husband means so much at the holidays and always" while listening to 50 Cent or murder podcasts. Later, I moved to the humor card team, where I'd hoped to eventually end up. This all sounds like a deleted scene from *500 Days of Summer* (probably the scene that had all the characters of color with dimension and backstories), but it was my honest-to-God life for about five years.

Like most nine-to-five, extremely corporate jobs, my day-to-day had boring parts and not fun parts and soul-suckingly frustrating parts. Those parts eventually became more frequent and weighed more heavily than the silly, dreamy, fart joke parts. I'd spent five years at a billion-dollar corporation with a few thousand employees, the majority of whom were well-meaning, white Midwesterners. As one of the few young, female, only-half-white employees, I'd heard enough conversations about "figuring out how to utilize Facebook" and "figuring out how to utilize feminism but without getting political" and "figuring out how to utilize multiculturalism—or is it called 'diversity' or are we calling it 'inclusivity' now? I can't keep up!!!" to last me the rest of forever.

I also wanted to start writing more. Both writing more frequently and writing more as in length. (Another insider tip: a "long" greeting card has maybe fifty words max, which is about how many words I prefer to use in exactly one sentence.) Plus, greeting card copy lives in this weird space: in terms of corporate writing, it is admittedly nice and beautiful. You get to spend your day figuring out how to put words to some of people's most personal, special, and intimate moments. But also, you're making money off of people's most personal, special, and intimate moments. Depending on how I was feeling on any given day, I got to/had to live in this timeless, arguably cultureless vacuum, where it was forever a special occasion. I had to make a product that the corporation deemed relevant to what was going on in the world but in a "don't mention any celebrities or specific brands" kind of way, and I couldn't be *too* time-specific, and also IS ANY-ONE EVEN BUYING GREETING CARDS ANYMORE??? I am very chill when it comes to existential crises.

So, when I got a Tumblr message from a creative executive at a local ad agency asking if I was interested in leaving my current job boyfriend to work for a new, shiny job boyfriend, I very casually orgasmed at the idea of change of any kind. (That's right, kids, Tumblr wasn't always just a social media platform for moody text posts and easily accessible porn gifs. It was where adults did business.) To put it professionally, I was extremely horny for something new. I felt stagnant and bored and saw no attractive path forward as a greeting card editor. But ~*The Ad World*~ was different and new and, did I mention, different!

And so, I left. I quit my stable, well-paying job, where I felt appreciated but underutilized, comfortable but worried I had stopped growing. I put in my two weeks' notice (which was actually a full month's notice . . . this greeting card bridge had treated me well and thus no greeting card bridge burning took place) to start working at the aforementioned ad agency where I'd been lured by the promise of writing! Full-time! I would be a full-time writer! Yum, yum, I ate the promise up with a #sponsored spoon.

I didn't know what quitting would be like, if not fiery and ferocious and filmed for a viral YouTube video. The actual act of quitting my greeting card job turned out to be very cordial and nice, and I definitely cried on multiple occasions but in a good way. I set up a meeting with my boss, and she was like, "Is this the meeting I think it is?" and I was like, "Yeah." And she was like, "Damn. Okay." The "meeting" was really just thirty minutes of us going back and forth saying how good of a boss/employee the other was. My boss was understanding and encouraging and remains my pinnacle of Good Managers/People. When I told my coworkers, they did that thing where they were like, "Happy for you but sucks for us," which makes me want to sob just thinking about it.* Because this was a Big Corporation, I also had to meet with my boss's boss and an HR person or two, but, thankfully, those meetings weren't awful. There was a little bit of "maybe we can make this work" and them asking if there was anything they could do for me to stay. It was admittedly flattering (and what human person doesn't love a little flattery), but I had already made my decision to leave (and also, I'd signed a contract with the ad agency).

Leaving felt scary and good and nerve-racking and right. When I drove out of the parking garage for the last time, I happy-sobbed while playing NSYNC's "Bye Bye Bye" with the windows down because I am, without a doubt, that bitch.

The previous summer, the summer of 2015, was another pivotal time for me. Over the course of a few months, I broke up with my boyfriend of almost four years, starting dating for the first time in almost four years, and met Riley, the person who is now my husband. What I'm saying is, when I fuck around, I don't fuck

---

* *Crying Because People Are Nice to Me* is what this book should have actually been called.

around, and it always leads to a very serious, monogamous relationship. ("Always" meaning literally just the once.)

The decision to end that four-ish-year relationship—my first Real Adult Relationship, which had seen me through the end of college, moving across the country, and most of my first Real Adult Job—was an incredibly difficult one. He was the first person who I felt loved by in a real, romantic way. He was good to me and to my family (extra admirable given my parents' extremely vocal, very Catholic disapproval at our decision to live together despite not being married). He was an overall good person. (We don't still keep in touch, but from the updates I squeeze out of our mutual friends—because I am nosy and want to know all things always—he is still an overall good person who has found another very good person to be married to.)

There was nothing classically "wrong" with our relationship. No one cheated. No one was intentionally hurtful or harmful. No one cut their sandwiches the wrong way or had a deep affinity for Dane Cook. Still, I grew more and more unhappy. Why does no one tell you that's how relationships can be: that nothing can be "wrong" but things can feel not "right"?

Oh, literally everyone says that? There are songs and novels and TV show subplots about it? It's just that I don't understand anything until it affects me in a deeply personal way? Gotcha.

In hindsight, I should have been more upfront about my unhappiness as it was growing. I shouldn't have waited until one afternoon while his parents were in town from out of state—I should clarify that I know that I, in no way, come out of this looking like the "good guy"—to tell him that I hadn't felt happy or satisfied by our relationship for a while, that our relationship felt more platonic than romantic, that I wanted to break up. He felt blindsided.

I didn't know what breaking up with someone would be like. I had never broken up with someone before. Not to brag, but all three of my middle school relationships ended with me being dumped by the guy or the guy's friend on AOL Instant Messenger. (Just thinking about the sound of someone signing off of AIM makes me break out in hormonal bacne.) In college, I had sort-of kind-of dated people in that way where you're like, "You want to be my boyfriend?" and they're like, "Let's not put labels on this." And you're like, "Cool, cool, love that. So, you'll just keep calling me when you're drunk and falling asleep while touching my boobs?" And they're like, "What did you say? I'm so drunk right now." There is no breakup conversation associated with those kinds of pseudo-relationships. They just fizzle out or you get old enough to realize you can fall asleep while honking your boobs all by yourself.

Our breakup was not fiery or ferocious; it was mostly just sad. Really, really sad. I know "sad" is a trite way to describe a breakup, but in its simplest form, that's how it felt. It's sad to want to comfort someone who you've made sad in the first place. It's sad to hear someone say, "Maybe we can make it work," and not have that feel comforting. (Instead of it easing a weight off my shoulders, it felt like a thousand Tim Gunns on my back.) I know this isn't even a little bit relatable or comforting to someone who has been broken up with recently or perhaps ever. I know initiating the breakup is supposed to culturally void me of my right to sadness as per rom-com and pop ballad rules. That's why the song is called "Someone Like You" and not "(I Left You for) Someone Like You (Only Better)." Still, it was hard and hollowed me out in a way I hadn't felt before.

Leaving felt scary and nerve-racking but right. I don't remember what I did the night he moved the last of his things out of our apartment.

The very first day at my Shiny, New Advertising Job was fun! And shiny! And new! The office had windows! I could work off-site! I was always within a ten-foot radius of a group of young people! We wore hats inside! This all seemed Disney World–level magical after working in an old, mostly windowless, corporately dressed office space for five years. I was wary of the advertising industry as a whole, but I remember telling people how excited I was to "work really hard!" I also remember telling myself that it wasn't complete bullshit that I was excited to "work really hard!" (Reader, it was complete bullshit.)

While I had desperately wanted to work on something new and challenging, I quickly realized I didn't want that new, challenging thing to be advertising. Specifically, ad copy for a candy bar. That was trying to appeal to Millennials™. Through, like, four-word Instagram captions. I learned this on about the second day of my rapidly dulling, still extremely new advertising job.

What's that thing where you don't realize you're living in your personal hell until it's suddenly 300,000 degrees and you're sharing a workspace with Satan? Is there a German word for it? Writing social media ad copy for a candy bar was a brand of hell catered specifically to me. It is not, of course, everyone's hell.

There were and are plenty of people who would have pushed me into the fiery depths for the position I had and the salary I had negotiated. If nothing else, I learned from my ad job that you always, *always* ask for more than they offer. There is probably more money and you definitely deserve it. Also, successful negotiation makes you feel powerful and sensual, like how I imagine Helen Mirren feels constantly.

If you've ever wondered who decides which emojis go into the copy for those sponsored Instagram posts you scroll past on your news feed, the answer is . . . LIKE, TWELVE DIFFERENT PEOPLE. At one point, I had to make a case for why puns were "on trend." My case was, "They aren't! I just like them! I was told I was going to be writing humor copy, but oops, surprise! I'm somehow spending my time talking to my Lit Instagram Fam #CandySquad *insert tongue sticking out emoji and/or fire emoji depending on which one you team of forty-year-old men think is more millennial*!!!" I had barely finished the first week before I was trying to figure out how long I had to stay for it to not be personally and professionally embarrassing when I left.

I didn't even last two months. My brief (but also somehow extremely long) eight-ish weeks devolved into working stupidly long hours on projects I cared stupidly little about. I was leaving early and coming home late. Seconds after stepping in the door at home, I would start furiously crying while shoving dinner into my mouth. I was spending most of my nights scream-sobbing to Riley about how much I hated what I was doing, and he was spending most of his nights asking me why I didn't leave. Then I'd scream-sob about how I was worried it was too soon for me to decide I needed to quit, and the scream-sob cycle would start over again. I was drinking! During! THE WORKDAY! A thing I had never even considered doing before and have never done since, let alone done on more than one occasion. Once, while home for a quick lunch break, I decided to chase my meal (a handful of Goldfish crackers while trying not to cry) with a shot of whiskey. I remember thinking, in my delusional state, "This is fine! This is normal and fine!" If you couldn't tell by the aforementioned workweek day-drinking and nightly scream-sobbing, it was not normal, and I was not fine.

I can't pinpoint the one or two reasons why I hated the job as much as I did. It was, in part, because it felt like a regressive step in my career: I was writing less of what I wanted to, instead of more; I was working on projects that I was both bored by and that made me feel gross instead of projects that, while boring, made me feel neutral or even a little good. I didn't feel valued. I didn't feel needed. I felt like my New Job Boyfriend had courted me and the second I said "yes," he was like, "LOL JK I am not a boyfriend but a stinky garbage dump! Ha ha, you just fucked a garbage dump!" To top this shit sundae with a rotten cherry: all of the intuitive wariness I'd had about entering advertising felt validated by the experience I was having. And so, after mustering up a stupid amount of courage, I decided I needed to quit.

Despite knowing I needed to quit, figuring out *how* to quit was way more difficult this time around. The conversation I repeatedly had with myself went like this:

"I need to quit."

"But you've only been there for, like, six weeks."

"Yeah, but it's been, like, five weeks and six days of me feeling miserable."

"But maybe it will get better?"

Both internal voices laugh in unison.

"But maybe you can last a year?"

"A YEAR?!?"

"But maybe you can last until the end of this year?"

"That's six more months. I don't even want to do six more days."

"But what will everyone at your new job say? And the people at your old job? And your friends and family and strangers who hear about how you quit your job for another job, and you lasted less than two months at that new job before quitting? What if they all think you're a failure and a quitter and bad at everything and you never get another job again?"

"I don't care what they'll say."

Both internal voices laugh in unison.

"I'll get through tomorrow and decide."

After having that conversation in my head daily, I started having it aloud with Riley. Then I started talking to my sister about it. Then I shared parts of my internal conversation aloud with the couple of people who I felt comfortable with at the ad job. Turns out, I was not even a little bit alone in how I felt. One of my coworkers, who was also pretty new and also pretty unhappy, described the environment as a "pressure cooker," and that's when both of the voices in my head were like, *Yeah, you need to leave.*

I set up a meeting with my manager via an email that was probably stilted and uncomfortable like, "Hello, we need to do a meeting very soon please thank you this is normal business I am doing normal business." When we met, my manager was like, "Is this the meeting I think it is?" and I was like, "Yeah." Our conversation was brief, much shorter than when I quit my greeting card job, but I still managed to cry. I cried partially out of embarrassment that I was leaving so soon (the idea of looking incompetent or like a failure to anyone is only what literally keeps me up at night!), but I mostly cried out of relief that I was finally having the conversation aloud with the person who needed to hear it. My manager expressed little surprise at my quitting and said I was more of a "writer's writer" anyway. I said thank you, like she meant it as a compliment. She was more of a "manager's manager."

The two weeks between that meeting and my last day were wildly uncomfortable. I took full advantage of working off-site. I left at five. I didn't wait in line for the office's weekly 4 p.m. Friday margaritas. My exit interview with HR was on what would have been my two-month work anniversary. When I left the parking garage for the last time, I didn't cry.

In late June of 2015, I was single, by my own doing, for the first time in four years. It felt fun! And shiny! And new! I had wine and cheese for dinner! I watched hour-long makeup tutorials on YouTube without headphones! I flirted with a barista who didn't flirt back! I was functioning on rumspringa-levels of sudden liberation, hurriedly trying to experience years' worth of dating in my twenties as quickly as I could. This feeling of "everything all at once" in no way speaks to my ability to dive, head first, into the proverbial pool. (I am much more a "dip a toe in, watch some people's reaction to the water, dip another toe in, assess the water from afar some more, finally decide to climb in right as the lifeguard's blowing the whistle to signal end of day" kind of person.) I mostly just didn't want to feel behind, dating-wise.

I signed up for Tinder! I deleted Tinder! I ran with my sudden desire to go out and stay out late on a weeknight! I knew the feeling of freedom would wear off as soon as I was by myself for more than a few moments. But in the meantime, I was conducting my own rom-com montage where I was trying on multiple floppy hats, if you know what I mean. (What I mean is that I literally bought a hat. Also, I fucked a bunch.)

I even had a Rebound! I mean, he was/is a human, but for the purposes of this anecdote, he was a Rebound. Rebound was different! And new! And did I mention different? Rebound made me feel sexy! Rebound made me feel wanted! Rebound bought a shitty $5 vibrator off Amazon after the first night we hung out because chivalry or something! I remember telling people how amazing it was to be a twenty-first-century human woman who could have a physical relationship without catching feelings. I remember telling myself that I wouldn't catch feelings. (Reader, I caught feelings.)

The feelings I caught were less about me wanting to have a serious, committed, or even defined relationship with Rebound and more about me realizing that Rebound was, in fact, a rebound. The shininess of dating again wore off. I quickly remembered that part of casual dating was sometimes people treat you shitty just because they can. I didn't feel valued. I didn't feel loved. I was starting to feel gross and bored instead of good or even neutral.

In recounting this story about Rebound to my sister, she said, "Yeah, you called me about him a lot. Like, every night." I don't remember doing that, but that sounds very me. I do remember crying about Rebound on more than one occasion and saying aloud, to myself, at least once, "What the fuck am I doing?" I probably saw him one or several times too many after that. Having someone who paid attention to me, even in small bursts, was admittedly flattering (and what human person doesn't love a little flattery), but I knew I needed to leave.

Our couple-week fling ended after I said something along the lines of, "This isn't fun for me anymore." (If nothing else, I learned that you should always, *always* use your stupidest, most rom-com-y lines on a Rebound. It will make you feel sensual and powerful like Helen Mirren.)

I don't remember the last time we hung out, but eventually I left. He kept the vibrator.

Riley and I met at the height of the aforementioned singleness rumspringa of 2015.

We had been dating for about nine months when I quit my greeting card job. That summer was one of the most challenging times in our relationship to date. He saw me through quitting one job, starting a new job, and hitting a low professionally and personally. He wished me well when I left too early in the morning and waited up with pizza when I came home too late at night. Despite my begging, he did not go into the ad agency, dressed up as me, and quit in a memorable but respectable way so I didn't have to. (I only love him a little bit less because of it.)

After quitting the ad job, I told him I wanted to start freelance writing full-time despite having, uh, less than a full-time load of freelance clients. (I had exactly zero.) He was realistic and encouraging and probably warier than he let on. Full-time freelance writing had been my ultimate goal, but it was happening sooner than either of us expected or than I intended. I was still testing the freelancing waters when Ad Job Me pushed us in like, "Bitch, get in the pool. We're literally on fire."

This is the part where I clarify that I was only financially able to jump in because of the five years I spent at my greeting card job. (That and the affordability of living in the Midwest. Come visit! Our rent is cheap, and you can get a beer for the low, low price of only ever seeing white people!) Working for that long at a Big Corporation, even one that makes greeting cards, helps create a nice, little money lifesaver to keep you afloat while you figure out the rest of your life.

After three-ish months of treading water, I was hired as a part-time writer for a women's website. Eventually, the fountain of rejection emails for my one-off humor pieces started spitting out a few acceptances here and there. As I write this, I am making nowhere near as much money as I was at my previous jobs and—surprise!—even Dream Jobs come with boring parts and stupid parts and parts where you're like, "This particular project feels regressive career-wise but also it is going to pay next month's electric bill." It's scary and nerve-racking and also the most satisfying thing I've done in my entire career. I don't remember how I celebrated the first time I got a piece accepted into a major publication, but I know that Riley was the first person I told.

On a Friday in the beginning of August 2015, while I was still editing greeting cards, Riley and I met. A mutual friend introduced us, even though I told her I wasn't interested in something serious. Riley was having people over at his house, and my friend said I should come with. So I downed half a bottle of wine, fully ready to give zero fucks about who I met and what they thought of me. (Reader, I gave all of my fucks about what Riley thought of me.)

Riley was new but familiar in the best kind of way. The four of us—me, Riley, my friend, and her girlfriend—spent the rest of that Friday laughing and drinking and talking. We listened to bad music and made bad jokes and tried to twerk upside down on a wall just to see if we could. (We couldn't.) Riley and I went to dinner on Saturday, just the two of us. After the first night we hung out, Riley bought me a full-size two-pack of contact solution, something that is meant to last over two months, to keep at his house. (Riley asked me to clarify that he has 20/20 vision. And if it wasn't abundantly clear, homeboy was ready to commit ASAP.) I don't remember when I finished the last of the second bottle, but it happened years ago. In the summer of 2018, we got married.

WORK ORIENTATION FOR WOMEN

Welcome to Big Company! We're all so excited you're joining the team. Just to be clear, our use of "excitement" is not, in any way, a euphemism. We've been told not to make those anymore as we don't want it to be construed as sexual harassment. Gotta keep up with the current cultural climate in a way that makes us seem self-aware but doesn't force us to grow or change! Ha ha, we have fun here.

Let's start by talking about what it means to be a part of our Big Company Family. Yes, we're not just a group of coworkers— we're a *family*. There are dads and grandpas and aggressive step-brothers and many uncles. Have you heard of *Sister Wives*? It's also kind of like that.

We chose *you* for a reason! So give yourselves a round of applause just for being here. We certainly have as it helped us reach a gender quota we've been told we aren't allowed to have in writing.

Diversity is so important to us at Big Company. You'll notice we like to say it at least once a meeting. Then everyone will nod and say, "Yes, so important," without actually agreeing to anything. As you're certainly aware, diversity can refer to gender, race, sexual orientation, religion, economic background, so many things! Our leadership represents a diverse background in recreational sports and a melting pot of J.Crew button-ups. Have you ever had white cheddar fondue? Okay, but what about with cocktail weenies? That's the kind of melting pot we're talking about.

Our company's done some soul-searching in the last couple of years. This involved HR shining flashlights into dimly lit cubicles, rifling through filing cabinets, trying to find at least one person with some semblance of a conscience, one male employee who hasn't done a Bad Thing. We're happy to say that we found a few!

All our current employees have undergone serious sexual-harassment training to teach them what is a prosecutable offense in our state, what will get them in trouble, and what HR will ultimately ignore. So, if you believe a coworker is acting inappropriately or you are receiving unfair treatment based on your gender, we promise you're not! Everyone here has sat through one thirty-minute PowerPoint, thus solving the harassment thingy altogether.

Where are the women under thirty-five? Hi there! You'll be getting a separate orientation regarding How to Deal with Older Male Coworkers Who Hit on You. There is no set time for this orientation. It will happen when you least expect it: sitting at your desk, leaving the bathroom, wearing a dress to the office for the first time. The orientation will be led by a man old enough to be your dad who will quickly try to assert himself as "cool." He will ask you questions like "Your boyfriend must be pretty proud of you. Wait, *you* don't have a boyfriend?" and "Are you really old enough to have a college degree? You look like you're still in high school!" You will feel like this orientation never ends, and trust us, it won't!

Women thirty-five and over, don't worry! No one will even pretend to be interested in you! And if they do, wow! What a compliment!

Let's get down to business—we are at work after all! We encourage you to #LeanIn! But please, make sure you're wearing an appropriate blouse. We value breaking glass ceilings provided you do so quietly and don't make too much of a mess. Ultimately, we want you to feel empowered to negotiate, to be assertive with your career trajectory, and to really go after it, you Girl Boss, you! Which we mean in a fun and colloquial way. There are no women at a senior level of leadership here.

COLLEGE 101

Introduction to College

COURSE MATERIAL:

- College map you pretend to not look at as you try and find where Room 408 in the science building is

- One or more of the following: a *Breakfast at Tiffany's* poster in your dorm despite never having seen *Breakfast at Tiffany's*; an acoustic guitar you only half-play; an idea of what college is based solely on movies and the internet

- An excited fear of what's next

After graduating from high school in 2008, I applied to exactly two colleges. Most of what I remember from the application process is my mom berating me to, for the love of God, finish writing my personal essays. I also distinctly remember crying in response, going to our shared family desktop computer, and writing posts on my blogger.com account that probably started *SoOoOo . . . I *should* be writing my personal essay for college apps right now . . .* and then writing five hundred words on why

Jesse McCartney, a Disney Channel–bred pop star with swoopy blond hair, was "like . . . weirdly hot to me."

Both universities I eventually finished applications for were small liberal arts schools in Wisconsin. One of them touted itself as the "Harvard of the Midwest." I have many friends and a husband who also attended the Harvard of the Midwest at universities located in Wisconsin, Missouri, Michigan, Illinois, Iowa, and Minnesota. Every school can be an Ivy League school if you get even one local paper to dub it as such.

I was happy to be done with high school. But the actual act of going to college was not something I had fully considered. The *idea* of things has always been much more exciting to me, a person who loves to say she is going to do a thing without actually having to do the thing. To paraphrase a popular quote: I hate writing; I love having written almost as much as I love having an impending project that I can spend all of my time telling people about rather than doing the actual project itself. It is a philosophy I have unfortunately applied to all aspects of my life, from going to parties to rearranging my living space to writing this very book.

Getting accepted into college was more a relief than anything else. I was pretty sure I ticked all the boxes required to get into a small school with a decent reputation: good grades, a list of extracurriculars, a summer in high school where I panic-considered playing tennis to seem more "well-rounded" on college applications, a middle-class upbringing where college is expected and in some ways taken for granted, regular community service hours, letters of recommendation from my biology teacher who called me "kind" and my science skills "middle of the pack," and a hurriedly written personal essay that reeked of teenage desperation.

I got accepted and was offered scholarships to both colleges, one of which I'd only applied to because my mom was like, *Hmm just a thought but maybe you should apply to a school that doesn't cost $40,000 a year?* The other school I applied to cost $35,000 a year. My student loans came with so many zeros it seemed like a joke, one I definitely didn't get until after graduation when I was like, "Oh, you want *me* to pay you back *that*?" After accepting the offer from one of the Harvards of the Midwest, I had to face my newest nightmare: actually having to go to college.

Guide to Roommates 101

COURSE MATERIAL:

- Three hundred Mac Photo Booth photos of you and your randomly assigned roommate

COURSE EXPECTATIONS:

- Passing this class depends solely on your ability to not do sex things in front of your roommate. Please, for the love of God, do not do sex things in front of your roommate.

I experienced a lot of firsts at Faux Harvard of the Midwest. It was where I moved into my first and only college dorm room. It was where I lived with my first and only randomly assigned roommate. It was the first time that I understood the joy of listening to Kate Nash's indie pop anthems on repeat as I walked to class. It was the first time I learned that not even Kate Nash could make me like college. It was, as foreshadowing would have it, the first of three universities I would attend throughout my collegiate career.

In September 2008, I moved into my dorm for the beginning of first trimester. (Yes, this school chose to divide its years into trimesters instead of semesters, which explains why it also had the audacity to charge $40,000 a year for tuition.) There, I met Hannah, my randomly assigned roommate and the first (and perhaps only) friend I made in college.

After filling out a roommate profile, answering questions like "Would you describe yourself as messy?" (*Is my mom looking, because then "ugh fine I guess yeah"*) and "Would you prefer a roommate who doesn't drink alcohol?" (*Is my mom looking, because then "for sure no def not"*), Hannah and I were assigned to each other. Who knows whether Admissions really sifts through hundreds of roommate profiles, playing OkCupid in order to find each student a perfect roommate match. However, that does sound like my exact brand of boring dream job right after naming racehorses and nail polish colors. All I know is that Hannah was the jackpot of this randomly assigned roommate lottery.

We both came from relatively conservative, pretty Christian upbringings. We were both slowly but surely realizing that our parents' beliefs didn't need to be our own. We both had younger sisters who we were obsessed with in a mostly normal, healthy way. We did not feel cool enough to make friends with the East Coast girls on our floor. We shared a secret love of the Jonas Brothers and a less-than-secret hate for the university we were both attending. We were a heavenly match made in college hell.

Partying at Parties 102

COURSE MATERIAL:

- A preconceived notion that college parties include red cups, teens going *WOO!*, and flips from rooftops into pools

COURSE EXPECTATIONS:

- Learning the difference between how Miller Lite smells and bad weed tastes

In my first (and only) trimester at Midwestern Harvard, I did have moments that felt like the "real college experience" I'd expected to have. One of my first weekends at school, I went to a party for a fraternity somehow related to horticulture or ecology or maybe it was all a ruse to grow pot in the greenhouse. I don't remember what I wore, but I do remember feeling underdressed in comparison to the Cool Girls from my dorm. I must have missed the part of the welcome packet that said slinky black dresses were a prerequisite.

The party, the first college frat party I'd ever attended, was held at a shitty house with a shitty basement. Just like the movies! My shoes stuck to the poorly kept hardwood floors, and none of the upperclassmen would make eye contact with me, despite my desperate efforts to eye-fuck anyone within my periphery. I made my way down to the basement where "music" was playing and people were "dancing." It was all flashing lights, thumping bass, and white people flailing their arms. Someone could have been banging their face on the lid of a trashcan and it would have sounded, looked, and smelled the same.

While still trying to get even one guy to look at me, I accidentally made eye contact with a stranger's butthole: a young man, likely intoxicated and definitely getting financial support from his parents, had taken off all his clothes (save for his socks but including his shoes) and continued dancing as if everyone were watching. I was surprised. I was aghast. I was disappointed that my view only included his butt and occasionally the back of his balls, scientifically, the worst part of the genitals. This was not how I'd expected my first encounter with an entirely nude male to go.

Eventually, the group I'd come with left the party. Not even the naked guy looked back at me.

Teachers Are Just People 201

COURSE MATERIAL:

- A strong desire to be liked by any and all authority figures

GRADE BREAKDOWN:

- Your grade will be dependent on your ability to form opinions based on—get this—your own ideas

In mid-December of 2008, I moved back home after deciding to transfer from Corn-Fed Harvard. (If nothing else, my freshman year of college should be legally recognized for its brevity.)

After barely three months at that school, I felt like I was (a) too dumb to attend even a fake Harvard and (b) accruing too much student debt to just feel so, so dumb. In hindsight, my grades were fine, but, for the first time in my academic career, I realized I had no idea how to study and hated feeling like I didn't understand a concept immediately. Based on my previous twelve years of schooling, I thought being a good student only entailed showing up to class, turning in assignments on time, and giving opinions that were just the teacher's regurgitated ideas couched with "thus" and "furthermore." I, someone who based a large part of her personality on the number of AP classes she took, didn't fully understand that you go . . . to school . . . to learn.

It took me a while to understand that I was allowed to form my own opinions, to realize the things I thought didn't need to be validated by a teacher or parent to be "good." It was something I still didn't fully understand as I finished out my freshman year commuting to and from a community college thirty minutes away from my parents' house. It was there, though, that I started to realize that maybe class instructors didn't know everything.

At the community college, I took Philosophy 101 because it was a general education requirement and it felt comfortably familiar to listen to older white men telling me how to think about the world. The professor was sweaty and Southern and liked to sit on his desk and EMPHASIZE words RANDOMLY. He spent one class talking about how he was "pro-life," polling the class on their thoughts on abortion. It was less a dialogue about the moral and philosophical quandaries related to abortion and more a chance for him to yell loudly from the edge of his desk. In another class, he talked about how ideas of beauty were cultural and that he, personally, did not find Pamela Anderson attractive. (Pamela Anderson could not be reached for comment.) He said that he, instead, found "people like Mia and Caroline attractive." He gestured to me and Caroline, my classmate who sat two seats down. I did not employ Socratic questioning, asking him to "explain further" or question "why the fuck he thought that was an okay thing to say."

During another class about cultural differences and philosophy—this professor loved to talk about "other cultures" in the context of words like "savage" or "barbaric"—he decided to employ me once again in a hypothetical situation. He did this with students often: *Let's say Danielle grows up in a religious household* or *What if Guy in the Front Row Who Always Wears a Racing Jacket decides to run for office.*

However, during this lesson's hypothetical scenario, I got *Mia is "female circumcised."*

The professor proceeded to explain a situation in which I was married to Walter, the student who sat next to me. In this hypothetical scene, I cheat on Hypothetical Walter, to which Actual Walter turns to me and goes, *How could you?!?* And Actual Me is like, *Not now, Walter.* Now, in this hypothetical culture, cheating is a legally punishable offense for women. So, Hypothetical Me gets her "clitoris scooped out" with "something like a melon baller," as my Actual, Real Life Philosophy professor explains, so that I can "never experience pleasure" ever again.

Now, is this right or wrong? the professor asked the class. I still don't know which scenario, hypothetical or actual, he was talking about.

College Hookups 301

COURSE MATERIAL:

- A sneaky condom from the front desk

- Enough pent-up horniness to jump on the first person who makes eye contact with you

PREREQUISITES—TO TAKE THIS CLASS YOU MUST HAVE COMPLETED THE FOLLOWING:

- Bad High School Make-outs in Your Parents' Basement 101

- Quietly Masturbating While You Pray to God Your Roommate Is Sleeping 202

- At least one foreign language course at the 100 level

After years of masturbating in silence, I had sex for the first time my senior year of college on my boyfriend's roommate's futon. It was fine. My sexual education in college was sporadic. I took Making Out 201: Does Kissing Someone's Neck Mean They Think You'll Give Them a Blow Job? I repeatedly failed Imaginary Relationships 501: Getting the Boy Who Calls Me Crying Every Night to Say I'm His Girlfriend. I also took a trimester-long elective called Romance 102: Inevitably Hooking Up with the Guy from Calc Who Keeps Texting You "when r we gunna hook up?" at One in the Morning.

You may also have taken this class if you've ever realized, after a thirty-minute conversation and fifteen minutes of making out, that the person you're hooking up with has a roommate and that roommate is currently asleep ten feet away from you. You've definitely taken the class if you still chose to spend the night anyway.

Graduation 401

COURSE MATERIAL:

- Student loan statements you try not to look at

- One or more of the following: a chunky sweatshirt with your university name; bad poetry from an introductory creative writing class you will hold on to for a little too long; half-memorized guitar chords to "Wonderwall"

- An excited fear of what's next

I eventually transferred for a second and final time to the university from which I have my degree. Sometimes I wish I'd had a more standard college experience. One with decidedly more pomp and circumstance, which is also what I call my left and right tits, respectively. I wonder who I'd be now had I spent my college years having weekend benders and late-night hookups and, well, just a little bit more fun. Other times, I'm just relieved to be done with the whole formal schooling thing. I graduated from college in three and a half semesters (*hold for applause*). This is less an example of my ambition and work ethic and more evidence of how much I like being done doing a thing. I hated going to college; I like being able to say I am a college graduate.

HOW I TAKE MY COFFEE

I used to take my coffee with cream. I was young and didn't understand things like "quality" and "strong brew" and "my own lactose intolerance." Life was so much simpler then.

Once, I dated a guy who took his coffee black so I started taking my coffee black. I would nod reflexively when he said things like "quality" and "strong brew" and "Isn't the mandolin in this song so good?" and "Did you come?"

Now I take my coffee very seriously, sniffing each individual bean and asking, "What will you make me capable of doing today, my small friend?" Maybe one day, when I've had too much caffeine or, more likely, not nearly enough, I will hear them reply.

Today, I take my coffee with a bagel. I say it like "bah-gel" and the cashier looks at me funny. I apologize and order a croissant instead. I don't even want to tell you how I pronounce "croissant."

I typically take my coffee in latte form. I get it with oat milk on account of not wanting to diarrhea to death. The way you order an oat milk latte is very specific. You go, "I'm so sorry but do you have oat milk and can I have that and again I am so, so sorry."

After a few minutes, I take my coffee from the shaggy-haired barista. Our fingers graze briefly as my hand meets the warm cup. I look up. He smiles. "Martha?" he asks. I laugh.

"It's pronounced *Mia*."

"No," he replies, "This coffee is for Martha." A woman pushes past me to grab her coffee. I ask if they have a coffee grinder I can shove my whole body into for just a sec.

Finally, they call out "Mya," and I take my coffee.

I take it to a table in the back, near an outlet where no one can sit behind me. God forbid someone sees me working or writing or googling "Pepsi girl how old now," which is, in a sense, working.

I take my coffee into my hands, sipping slowly at firs—oh fuck, fuck shit, that is so, so hot oh my god I barely even touched it to my mouth and now I've lost my entire bottom lip.

Some days, my coffee takes me. We dance in a caffeine frenzy around the café, swirling together in a flurry of brew and body. We move as one. I don't know if I am more her or she is more me. We laugh. We sing. "I take you as you are," my coffee whispers to me. I weep a single tear. It tastes like espresso and salt.

I take my coffee to go.

PROCRASTINATION BUT
MAKE IT LOOK PUT TOGETHER

I am a slut for procrastination. Spending days doing absolutely nothing, when I know I have many things to do, is perhaps the greatest love of my life. (Sorry to my husband, family, et al.) I will continuously put off whatever mandatory task needs to be done, coming closer and closer to the quickly approaching deadline, until I am eventually on my knees reciting the Procrastination Lord's Prayer:

> *Our Father*
> *Or Mom or Grandma,*
> *Stepdad or Great Aunt,*
> *Estranged Brother or Half-Sister,*
> *Younger Cousin Who Is Somehow*
> *Taller Than Me Now,*
> *Or Zaddy or Fuckboy or Grandma*
> *oh wait I said that already . . .*

The prayer ends when I run out of relatives I can name or I'm a day out from my due date. No forgiveness is granted. I am led straight into temptation. Then I spend a hurried twenty-four hours panic-working, trying to put together some semblance of whatever it is I should have been doing for the past week or month or twenty-eight years. It's like sexual edging but for responsibilities. And I do finish, eventually.

This is not some cutesy attempt at being Relatable™. Like, "Ha ha, look at me! I'm such a silly mess of a woman! Isn't it funny when women are messy but only if they are hot and young, too?" (I am, of course, very hot and perpetually young, but that is beside the point.)

I don't know when calling yourself a "hot mess" became a whole personality, but I do feel like it corresponds with our collective love of talking about procrastinating. Procrastination is gross (at least in terms of being a productive human person), and we all love to talk about gross things. We love to huddle around our icky shit pile of an id, *oohing* and *ughing* over its icky shittiness. It's the "Smell this and tell me if it smells bad" effect but for coping with our inability to cope.

People love to talk about procrastination if only as a way to further procrastinate whatever it is they should be doing. If I wanted, I could probably build an entire Etsy shop stocked with screen-printed T-shirts that say "I'd rather be procrastinating" and novelty mugs emblazoned with "Don't talk to me until I've had my procrastination." You can go ahead and steal those ideas from me. Just know if you make a million-dollar fortune off my intellectual property, I will come for my 15 percent. Yes, I even procrastinate my creative integrity.

It just feels so, so good to not do something you are told to do. It is the whole reason I became an English major. John Mulaney has a joke about how he spent $120,000 to have someone tell him to read *Jane Eyre* and then he didn't. I have a joke where I just rewatched John Mulaney's Netflix special to find that exact quote when I could have very easily googled it, but I kept thinking, *Maybe I'll get inspired to be funny if I watch hours of someone else doing it???* I'll think of a punch line eventually.

I do not wish to be this way, in a constant state of procrastination. I wish I always spent my self-designated work hours actually doing work instead of doing . . . I honestly don't even know what. If someone were to look at my daily schedule and try to figure out what my job is they would say, "Changing from one set of pajamas into another set of pajamas, staring at her dog, and eating string cheese while staring at a blank Google doc?" The amount of time I actually spend typing words is humiliatingly small. My ego drives a cherry red Porsche to compensate for it.

Yet I refuse to grow or change. I continue to procrastinate because I like it. I like it because, while it is happening, it feels really, really good. However, I am equal parts "hedonistic goblin" and "people-pleasing chameleon," and how I think other people see me is perhaps my greatest motivator. I want to do absolutely nothing, and then I want to be recognized for all my hard work.

This is a habit I've been feeding since elementary school. That is when I first felt the joy of being given a task, not doing it until it was absolutely, undeniably necessary, and still getting praise from the teacher. The habit grew hungrier in middle school when I'd complete assignments in study hall immediately before class and still fare better than my classmates. It grew ravenous in high school when I learned I could write a full paper the night before it was due and still get a relatively good grade. The habit, now as much a part of me as arms or my teeth, solidified in college. This was when I declared myself an English major, said quietly to myself, "I will not read even one single book," and proceeded to scrounge up lukewarm but professor-pleasing takes based off back covers and SparkNotes. College is where some people's procrastination goblins go to die. It is where mine grew a second head.

As that goblin grew, so did my desire to be loved and adored or, at the very least, seen as "nice." Not for any reason in particular, aside from maybe the fact that I am a Midwestern, half-Asian woman. So niceties, submissiveness, and pleasantries are my presumed personality, but I DIGRESS.

It is with absolute shame that I say I didn't question much (religion, politics, why boys I liked wouldn't touch me, why seeing boobs made me want to touch myself) until I graduated from college. Until I was about twenty-one, I would form and voice opinions based on the people around me, and my hobbies adhered to whoever I was in love with at the time. In third grade, I wanted to be a vet because that's what my best friend, Becky, wanted to be. In seventh grade, I learned *The Simpsons* theme song on the piano because the boy I liked (who would eventually become my "boyfriend" for two weeks and dump me over AOL Instant Messenger) often quoted the show. As a freshman in college, I thought about learning the rules of hockey because the only boy who expressed interest in making out with me played hockey. (I didn't learn about hockey. I did make out with him. Baby steps.) If you could procrastinate having a full personality, I was doing that at the whim of the people-pleasing lizard monster I was growing inside of me.

At the second of the three colleges I attended—yes, of course, my love of procrastination applied to figuring out what I was going to do with my life—I took a public speaking class. It was a general education requirement I'd eventually need to complete. So, for once in my life, I decided not to put off something that would be inevitable.

Something you need to know about me is I was always, *always* the person whose report card read, "Has good ideas but needs to speak up more in class." My internal Molotov cocktail of self-consciousness, anxiety, and general fear of looking stupid would build inside me during class. Any class: math, English, tech ed when I cut my finger open on a coping saw and was like, "Do you think it would bother the teacher if I told her I'm bleeding?" I could never get myself to speak up. When the bell would ring, I would combust silently in the back row, middle seat, both angry that I once again spent an hour saying nothing and relieved that I could finally be done waiting for myself to say nothing and leave. Needless to say, public speaking was not my forte.

I will call my college public speaking professor "Mr. Y" because that sounds anonymous and also kind of sad for some reason, which—honestly?—perfectly encapsulates him. Mr. Y was a very gentle man in every sense of the word. He spoke gently. He moved gently. He just had a general presence that made you feel like, *Shh quiet, baby is sleeping.* I don't remember Mr. Y being a particularly good teacher. This isn't to say that he wasn't or isn't a good teacher; it's just that I honestly remember very little of what he taught. Maybe that speaks for itself.

Mr. Y started off our very first public speaking class by telling us a little bit about himself. So little, in fact, that I really only remember him (our public speaking teacher) telling us (the public speaking class) that he had a deep, deep fear of public speaking (the subject he was teaching right now at that moment). He did not say that he previously, in the distant past, was afraid of public speaking and now he was on the other side of that fear, here to tell his tale of triumph. He made it very clear that public speaking was still something he very much feared. So much so, he said, that fear may at times prevent him from coming to class. The public speaking class. That he was teaching.

In some ways, I respected his honesty. I applauded his vulnerability and willingness to share what clearly affected him on an intimate, personal level. I both admired and envied his ability to tackle the thing he feared head-on, working through it in a direct and inescapable way. I am a greedy skank for other people's secrets, and I felt privileged to be gifted with one of his. In other ways, this was a college course I was paying money for which added to my growing student debt so, like, maybe this wasn't the best form of exposure therapy. The class was unconventional, to put it, as Mr. Y would, gently.

When a student gave a speech, Mr. Y and two of our classmates would grade the speech. We were graded out of five points on things like content and clarity. Mr. Y did this evaluation-by-committee as an effort to grade fairly. However, a thing about college students grading other college students is that none of us were super good at grading on account of . . . we were all students. No one in the class was getting an A, which had less to do with actual performance and more to do with student graders whose entire feedback was, "I just don't feel like it was a 5 but it was still really good!:):)" The only critique I remember getting over the course of the semester was from a fellow female student who suggested that I "maybe wear a necklace next time." To this day, I still don't know what the fuck that meant.

Because the class average was so low, Mr. Y offered an unlimited number of extra credit assignments to anyone who wanted to bring their grade up. The assignments involved writing summaries on chapters in the public speaking book he had us buy but never actually assigned as reading. Put another way, the infinite extra credit for this public speaking class involved no actual public speaking. I did the extra credit, obviously.

Since I knew I could easily make up for any poor speech grade, my motivation to work on my speeches dwindled. I would write my speeches the day before class, the night before class, the morning of class. A low point came when I still hadn't started writing my speech and I was due to present in two hours. Rather than doing the normal and sane thing of trying to write some semblance of a speech or asking for an extension, I devised a plan.

Our speeches required and relied heavily on a visual component. (Again, it wasn't really the best public speaking class.) I decided I would go to class, speech nowhere close to prepared, and wait until I was called to the front. Then I would walk up, confidently and completely normal like, "This is the good and fine walk of someone who has done her assignment on time and is ready to present." I'd hand my professor a CD-ROM upon which I'd scrawled in Sharpie something like "Mia Mercado Speech Final Draft 2." (This was 2009. Google Drive was but a twinkle in Silicon Valley's eye.)

I would watch Mr. Y put the disc into his desktop computer. I would watch the disc get spit out. I would look confused when he would try to put the disc in again and the computer would come up with an error message that read: "Disc empty." I would shrug and feign confusion like, "Sorry, Professor Who Is Thirty Years Older Than Me and Definitely Didn't Grow Up with This Technology. Me don't know computers either!!!"

I would nod when he suggested that perhaps it was a computer error and follow him to his office to see if he could get it to work there. I would walk a few steps behind him, just in case the cadence of my feet gave me away. (*Do I normally walk heel-toe or toe-heel or sashay sideways or backbend into a crab walk or roll like the hard-boiled egg of a human I am?!?*) I would watch as he put the disc into a second computer, mimicking panic as it continued to come up empty. "I swear it was working on my computer!" I would lie.

The whole time I would be well aware that I, an adult person paying hundreds of human dollars for this course, had just handed my college professor a blank CD. I would know full well that the PowerPoint had not been started, let alone completed and burned correctly onto the CD. I would know that he, a gentle and sympathetic person, would feel bad and let me do the presentation the next class session without docking me any points for being late. I would get away with it completely unscathed save for the residual feeling of guilt that I'd carry with me until I died.

If you're waiting for the twist, there is none. I brought in the blank CD. My professor believed that there'd been an error in transferring the files. He bought my feigned panic, and it cost me none of my "I'm a good student, please think I'm a good student" reputation. *He* may have even apologized to *me* in the process. I finished writing the speech that night, saved the PowerPoint onto a CD (as I'd done correctly dozens of times before), and presented it at the next class. I probably got a three out of five on my speech. I probably made up for it in extra credit. I think I got an A in the class.

The thing about real life is sometimes your stories don't have any immediate moral. Sometimes you chalk something up as a triumph and then immediately try to forget about it. Sometimes you sit in the back seat of your mom's car, years later, half-laughing about the time you tricked your teacher, and your sister says, "Oh my god, *you did that*?" Sometimes you ignore that sour stomach feeling of regret for two, three, ten years. Sometimes you take a literal decade to finally reexamine those stories, to replay your self-proclaimed victories, to pause at a moment you only now realize was pivotal. Eventually, you sit quietly through your life's credits wondering, "Who did I really defeat?"

Mr. Y, in all his gentleness, was not stupid. Kindness and sensitivity don't automatically render someone inept. I wish I'd learn to adopt his quiet compassion. I wish I realized sooner that most teachers want you to evolve, not acquiesce. I wonder if he knew I'd given him a blank CD. I wonder how he remembers me, if he thinks of me at all.

MY DOG EXPLAINS
MY WEEKLY SCHEDULE

My dog is named Ava. She is a four-year-old Havanese, which is the kind of dog that looks like a cotton ball came to life. She is my coworker in that I work from home most days and that is where she resides every day. She is perfect, and if you met her, you'd love her almost as much as she would love you. Here, in her own words, is what I do on a weekly basis.

It is a Monday. Or maybe a Wednesday. I, a dog, have no real sense of time. All I know is that She has put on a good smell, which means She is leaving. She only does this in the rare moments when She leaves. Thus, it is time for me to Panic-Whine.

She says "Go" and "Sorry" and puts on Shoes that I know are for Outside. She doesn't touch my Leash. I do a sad Lie Down in a fluffy blanket. I wait for somewhere between an hour and three lifetimes.

When She comes Home, She smells like Outside and carries something that looks like Food. "Coffee," She says and I sniff.

"No," She says and I still do a sniff but more sad. She picks me up and I wag. She knows I can't stay mad.

She sits at Table, which means I can't Sit in her lap. I realize then that I need to Sit in her lap. I say this again and again until She lets me Sit in her lap.

She carries me to a different spot: the Man Chair. This is the chair where Man sits when he comes Home. Most days, Man leaves and then comes back. She doesn't. She stays with me to stare at screens and eat Food and watch screens and talk to me and Sleep and look at a little, second screen in front of the main screen and Lie Down and Go Pee Pee and that's all.

Today is Bed Day. I love Bed Day! That's the day of the week where we both get to Lie Down and Lie Down and sometimes Pee but mostly Lie Down until Man comes home. Some weeks have one of these days. Some weeks have more. This is the second Bed Day this week.

She turns on Bath. I hide. She gets in Bath. I miss her already. I go to the basket and get Stink Underwear. I bring it up on the Bed with me to keep me company while She is in Bath.

She gets out of Bath and starts to put on Good Smell under arms. This means She is leaving but for a longer time. Maybe this means I will Go, too! I get very happy and excited. We could be going anywhere! To the Car! A Drive-Thru which gives me

Treats! To the Backyard! To a Park! To another Drive-Thru for Treats! Anywhere!

She grabs a bag but not my Leash. I am so, so sad. I am betrayed. I will not eat. I will not drink. I will sleep and make my eyes sad and that is all. I sit on Bed inside and watch her go to the Car outside. She is gone.

I miss her already!!! I panic and go to the basket. I get every Stink Underwear I can find with my tiny, little baby corn teeth. Some Stink Underwear is connected to Pants but that is OK. I will make a Shrine and Lie Down in it and not rest until She comes Home.

I wake up to the sound of the Door. (Okay, so I must have done a tiny rest.) I bark really scary and big (I am eight entire pounds!) until I see She is home! I do a tiny pee because I am so excited and because She will see my Stink Underwear Shrine!

Today is a Half Bed Day. This is like regular Bed Day, but instead we move to Couch eventually. She looks at her screen a lot today. I sit on her lap so I can see the screen, too. She moves me away. I love this game! She says something Happy and Good and my whole body becomes one big Wag. She puts her face near my face and I try to eat her Stink Mouth Air. She says "no" but not Very Angry. I try to sit back on her lap. We repeat this until Man comes home.

She gets up. Goes to Bath. I get Stink Underwear. Same routine, different Day. She puts on a Good Smell, gets a bag and my Leash, puts on her Shoes.

Wait . . . my LEASH!!! We are going Outside! I dance and dance and wag and dance. She takes me Outside and I get into the Car with her. We could be going anywhere! Every time the Car slows down, I try to stick my entire body out the Window in case it is a Drive-Thru for Treats. She puts the Window up higher, and I smoosh my snoot against the glass and sniff.

The Car stops. She goes Outside but I am still in the Car. I bark and whine because She forgot me, I am sure. After a long, long time or maybe only seconds, She walks around to the other side of the Car and lets me out. I Smell and Walk and Run and mostly Walk. She holds my Leash so She doesn't get too far away from me.

I don't know where we are or what we are doing, but I already like it here. Wherever She is, I like it.

Part 3

ON BEING
Domestic
AND
Beautiful

These are stories on faking your way through beauty, fashion, and homemaking. Or maybe you're not faking. Maybe you walk well in heels and are the only person who can keep a strapless bra up. Maybe you know how to make a pie crust from scratch and own at least one apron. Maybe you have pretty hair in the places where you're supposed to have pretty hair. It's weird that any of us are expected to be good at these things.

MUSTACHE LADY

The second time I realized I was hairy, I was ten and in the changing room of a juniors' clothing store with my mom and younger sister. "Maybe I should teach you how to shave your armpits," my mom said, noticing the tuft of hair peeking out below the capped sleeves of the shirt I was trying on. We'd come to this particular store because it's where Brittany S. had found the cool top she always wore, and I, too, wanted to be cool like Brittany S. All the Cool Girls I went to school with were named Brittany or Lindsay or any of the one million spellings of either name. I was the only Mia (this was 1999, before I shared a name with millions of toddlers and lap dogs across the country), and being different, as per Extremely White Elementary School rules, was not something that made me cool. I had not gone to Fashion Bug, this Midwestern mecca of preteen clothing, for a turning point in my adolescent life; I went for an ill-fitting gingham shirt with a popcorn bodice and capped sleeves. However, I only left with one of the two.

Not to toot my own puberty horn, but I was something of an early bloomer. By fifth grade, I was already sprouting mad armpit hair and had a small collection of bras that were less supportive garments and more something to flatten the weird little boobie buds my body had started forming. Pre-boobs are, to put it scientifically, very hilarious. It's like you wake up one morning and your nipples are just like, "Hey, you know what would be fun? If I looked like I was drawn by a cartoon artist. Watch—I'm gonna turn myself into these slightly oblong, lowercase *c*'s. Yay! Fun!" I don't remember being either excited or embarrassed by my boobs. They felt inevitable, like how my fingernails would get longer or my shoe size would change regardless of what or how often I thought of it. My body hair, though? Definitely not something I wanted any attention drawn to whatsoever.

The first time I realized I was a Hairy Girl, I was in third grade. A boy named Christopher J., whose body weight was 90 percent bowl cut, took to commenting on the dark hair above my lip to pass the time during social studies lessons. "You've got a mustache," he would say. Of all the ways to berate a person's body hair, this was perhaps the laziest. Like, no shit, I've got a mustache. I'm half-Filipino and my body is getting ready to fuck me up with puberty hormones. Also, maybe you haven't noticed, but I am what you call a human, and humans are covered head to toe, crease to chin, with body hair. You ever look at your toe knuckles? Like, *really* look at your toe knuckles? There's hair there, my dude. What evolutionary need do we have for hairy toe knuckles? Who knows! Probably the same need as my hairy upper lip. So why don't you mind your own hairy toe knuckles and turn that bowl cut around, Chris J.

Of course, I did not tell him that. I went home and told my mom what he said, and cried.

My life has been surrounded by fairer-haired, lighter-skinned friends. I remember Brittanys and Lindsays in high school complaining about how thick they thought their arm hair was, detailing the process of shaving their forearms and asking each other to "feel how smooth!!!" their arms were after shaving earlier that week. Not to play Oppression Olympics: Body Hair Edition, but if I shave my armpits at night, there will be stubble in the morning.

I have always had a weird relationship with my hair. It has been societally deemed my best and worst feature. Long, luscious hair on top of my head? Good! Beautiful! Would pay money for! Long, luscious hair on my legs, around my belly button, and on my upper thighs? Bad! Terrible! Would pay money to never have to see! Whenever people say they wish they had hair like mine, I say that they can for the low, low price of having more pubes than they know what to do with.

My mom taught me how to shave shortly after that trip to Fashion Bug. We bought a pack of pink disposable razors and store-brand shaving cream scented like some nondescript, alcoholic berry that would get you drunk enough to forget the state capitals. When we got home, she introduced me to the female ritual of Shaving.

She showed me how to wet my underarm skin a little first, how much shaving cream to squoosh out into my hand, how to gently spread it around my armpit. She showed me how to hold your arm up enough so your skin would be taut, how to shave with and against the grain—both are necessary when braving the forest that is my armpit. (Multiple coarse hairs grow out of each follicle under there. It is a personal bodily feat that is impressive to no one except myself.) My mom helped me wash away the foam and fallen hairs, both swirling down the drain until there was no trace of this undeniably weird yet completely normal ceremonial ritual we'd just performed. It's equally strange to talk about an act that my mother taught me out of love and that I continued doing out of hate for parts of myself.

Later that week, I tried to shave my legs for the first time—"try" being the operative word here. It was, to put it gently, a massacre. I abided by all the rules my mom had given me for Shaving 101, not realizing she had only given me the tutorial on Armpits, intentionally trying to shield me from noticing the dark hair covering my legs. I'd already noticed, though, and thought I'd get an early start on ridding myself of these thick, little sprouts that had taken up residence on my lower half.

What I didn't realize was that the amount of shaving cream you need varies according to the body part. Not sure why I didn't realize that: legs very clearly have more surface area than armpits. I was in the Gifted program for math (thank you, please hold your applause) and somehow I thought, "This li'l dollop will be good for all body parts large and small!" I also was unaware of the variables in play while applying pressure to your razor. Under your arm is fleshy and soft and harder to nick. Your shins, though? Oh, baby. Shins are Nick City. Shins are like the bridge troll of the legs, like, "Come, if you dare, try to navigate these boney peaks covered in the thinnest, most delicate layer of flesh! Test your knowledge of grooming on my labyrinth of patchy hair and bones!" Knees are even worse, but I didn't get to my knees the first time I shaved.

The very first swipe of my razor removed my leg hair as well as the thin, top layer of skin on my shins roughly a quarter of an inch wide and four inches long. I remember looking at my razor and thinking, "Huh, I don't remember my shaving cream having long, thin chunks in it?" When I looked back down, there was more blood than leg.

My mom was mortified. Not by the blood—my mom, a mother of four, has seen more bodily fluids than the black light in *Room Raiders*. However, the sight of your fifth-grade daughter bleeding from a self-inflicted shaving wound while essentially saying, "Mommy, do I look pretty?" is basically a scene from a horror movie. She helped me patch my leg up, apologizing over and over again for not teaching me that shaving my legs and armpits wouldn't be exactly the same. To this day, I think she still blames herself a little for what was entirely my overzealous doing. If anything, she should've been more disappointed in my public school math and science education. (Seriously, how did I not realize that Leg is bigger than Armpit???)

I spent the next two years (from fifth grade to halfway through middle school) too terrified to use a razor to shave. So I stopped shaving altogether, and here I am, a fully Evolved Woman basking in my body hair.

Just kidding! Instead of using sharp blades to get rid of my body hair, I turned to literal chemicals!!! Nair became my best, most stinkiest friend. If you haven't ever had the honor of Nairing, bless your hairless soul. It is a pinkish cream that smells like a rotten fruit came to life and puked in your face. You apply the cream to the hair you want removed, let it sit for a while—but not too long or it will give you literal chemical burns! Being a woman is fun!!!—and watch as each strand curls up into this wavy, dead, wiggle of a hair follicle. Then you wipe away your dead wiggle hairs and are left with smooth, gorgeous, stinky skin. Just describing this gave me flashbacks to sixth grade, when I clogged the toilet with Nair-soiled toilet paper. As I said, being a woman is FUN.

Eventually, I started using a razor to shave again. Time heals all wounds. Except the ones left by a disposable razor, as evidenced by the faint seventeen-year-old scar on my leg. Shaving with a razor again was like going back to an old boyfriend who I knew wasn't good for me, but everyone else was like, "But you're soOoOo cute together!!!" What can I say, I was in seventh grade and sick of wiping gross, pink Nair gunk off my upper thigh. So I ran back into the arms of my Bad Boy Razor.

Around the same time I started shaving again, I became reacquainted with a nickname I had been given years before: A boy in my seventh-grade class began each day by addressing me as Mustache Lady. *Good morning, Mustache Lady. How's it going, Mustache Lady? Hey, Mustache Lady, fine weather we're having.* At least I had been given a title this time around. I was a Lady. Mustache Princess or Duchess of Mustache would have been preferable, but I took what I could get.

I wish I could say that this nickname didn't bother me. That I ignored this dumb, dumb boy and his bad, bad insults. That I had been made wiser by the years between Christopher J. first pointing out my upper lip hair and this new boy dubbing me Mustache Lady. That I had been hardened by years of leg shaving and other body-hair removal. At this point, my body hair had caused me blood, tears, and Nair chemical burns. Whatever harm the nickname "Mustache Lady" had meant to do to me, I had already done to myself tenfold.

I wish I could say I definitely didn't cry to my mom when he called me that. I wish I could say I didn't immediately look into whether shaving your upper lip would make the hair grow back darker. I wish I didn't know that they make Nair specifically for upper lip hair removal, that I didn't know exactly how long to leave it on to get rid of the hair without causing my skin to become red and tender (four minutes and thirty seconds).

I wish I could say that, today, I don't even remember the name of the boy who called me Mustache Lady, what he looked like, or anything about him. I wish I could say that I, a twenty-eight-year-old adult woman, remember nothing of thirteen-year-old Justin K. with the frameless glasses and gelled spiky hair and his painfully uncreative teasing. I wish I could say my current Google search history doesn't include "eyebrow threading hurt more than wax or no." But I can't.

I shaved my mustache this morning, in the year 2020, as a financially independent, fully grown, adult woman. It has become as routine as putting on deodorant and brushing my tongue until I gag a little. (Maybe if my breath is minty fresh, no one will notice the hair that grows extra quickly around the corners of my lip?!?) It's not like I recite the names of all the boys who've insulted my facial hair as I complete this task, even though I can easily call their names to mind: *Christopher J., Justin K., College Guy Who Said I Had "Stubble" but Not in a Way That Sounded Impressed.* This routine would probably be a lot more satisfying if I did, though.

My younger sister—also a fully grown, adult woman—once told me she plucks her upper lip hair as her preferred method of hair removal. My response was not to immediately tell her how painful that sounded, to ask how long such a tedious and terrible task took. I did not give her older sisterly advice, telling her to preserve her precious youth by not bothering with upper lip hair, to live and laugh and, yes, even love. My response was to be jealous. I WAS JEALOUS! THAT MY SISTER! ONLY HAD ENOUGH UPPER LIP HAIRS! THAT SHE WAS ABLE! TO PLUCK THEM! INDIVIDUALLY!!!

Not to partake in the second annual Oppression Olympics: Body Hair Edition, but if I tried to pluck my upper lip hair, the first half would start growing back before I had time to finish the second. After that conversation with my sister, I thought about trying to pluck my mustache. When I stood, tweezers in hand, looking at the teeny forest above my upper lip, I audibly laughed, and my reflection looked at me and went, "You truly are a crazy li'l bitch, aren't you?"

Cultural beauty standards and expectations of femininity and women in movies who lifted their arms up and had smooth, hairless, light pit skin, have taught me to tie self-awareness to shame. I've been trying to undo or at least examine the things I've allowed, subconsciously or not, to seep into my daily routines. It's not like I spend all my waking moments thinking about all of the weird places my female body has decided to grow hair, though I can easily call each of these hairs to mind: the single hair on my chest I am convinced is a pube gone rogue, the armies of nipple hairs that guard my areolae, the one chin hair that happens to grow in the exact same place as my mother's one chin hair. How do I acknowledge each of their presences without implying that they are gross or weird or bad?

I don't know if I'll ever *not* be hyperconscious of my upper lip or the razor burn bumps around my bikini line or the discoloration under my armpits from my dark-haired stubble. I don't know if it would be better to have *never* been aware of these things: how my life would be different if I never knew to worry about my fingers being "too hairy for a girl" or wonder whether my butt crack was extra hairy or the normal amount of hairy. I don't know if I wish my mom hadn't told me I should start thinking about shaving my armpits in the dressing room in fifth grade. I don't know if it was too soon for me, personally, or too late for me, societally. I don't know how I will talk to my hypothetical future daughters about their own body hair, how I will weigh that delicate balance of helpful and harmful my own mother was so concerned about.

There is one thing, however, I do know for sure: I'm glad my mom didn't let me buy that Cool Girl shirt from Fashion Bug. By any and all beauty standards, it was ugly anyway.

I'M A GUY'S GIRL

Oh, I didn't see you there—I was too busy watching sports and shotgunning beers. I'm a pretty typical tomboy. Also, I'm pretty. It's confusing, I know. People are always like, "Were you created in a lab?" And I'm always like, "I'm not at liberty to discuss that."

Kidding! I love humor. Nothing is funnier to me than a boy fart or saying "pussy" for no reason. And, yes, you can swear around me. I'm used to it because I grew up with a bunch of brothers. It was so many brothers but also a normal number. Like, seventeen? Does that sound right?

I've always been a guy's girl. I love meats and video games and how gasoline smells and tires taste. You know—just dude stuff. I've never been into girly things like makeup or being culturally conditioned to hate my body. What even is "bronzer" or "eyelashes"? I don't understand why girls take so long to get ready. I put my human flesh on one leg at a time, just like one of the guys.

Girls are always so jealous and sensitive about everything. I don't get that. I literally feel nothing except interest in whatever you like. I don't think I'd get along with girls if I ever met one in real life.

Boys are just easier to hang out with. I guess that's what makes me a guy's girl. Specifically, the girl of some guys who created me during a thunderstorm. They glued two basketballs to a flagpole, waited for lightning to strike, and here I am.

Joking! Oh my god, you should have seen your face. You were like that guy from that movie you're so good at quoting. You remind me of Ryan Gosling, but I'd actually have sex with you.

Was that too forward? I don't want to come on too strong. But you know what they say: "Don't be a fucking tease like Lisa." That's the saying, right? I love sayings. Is now when I show you my basketball boobs? I mean, do you want to play basketball? Ha ha, I'm such a guy! Except I'm a girl!

Other girls are like, "Why are we being pitted against one another for the gratification of the male gaze?" But I'm like, "Because when we're against each other, our boobies touch and it's cool, duh." Speaking of cool, a cool thing about me is that my butt is just for decoration and that's all.

Ever since I can remember, I've always been more into guy stuff than girl stuff. My memory only spans the length of a day and restarts every morning because I'm just chill like that. I'm so good at chilling with the guys that Flip Cup is my middle name, which is funny because I don't even have a last name. Do girls have last names?

I thought I met a girl once, but she was just a maple-syrup bottle. We sat across from one another in the kitchen and quietly kept each other company. Neither of us spoke because there were no boys in the room for us to fight over. I thought about bringing her to life in a lightning storm so that I'd have someone to listen to me. But that'd be selfish—I wasn't brought here to think only of myself. I was brought here to think only of myself in relation to men.

Plus, I didn't have any basketballs to glue to her.

NATIONAL AMERICAN
MISS PRE-TEEN WISCONSIN

Soon after I hit puberty, I got a letter in the mail saying I was eligible to participate in a statewide beauty pageant. It was as if my period had sent a press release to the world announcing my coming of age.

> *(August-ish, 2001—Grafton, WI) Menses is excited to announce Mia Mercado kind of has boobs now and is technically fertile. She has affirmed to her mother that she "totally" knows what sex is, adding, "Ew." (We have yet to confirm from Mia whether she does, in fact, know what sex is.) We look forward to the confusing horniness she will experience, and welcome the onslaught of inappropriate sexualization she will inevitably face. Also, she's twelve! Further questions can be yelled to Mia through a bathroom door as she tries to figure out which part of the tampon stays inside of you and which gets thrown away.*

Like American males are required to register for the draft at eighteen, I was enlisted to serve my country through choreographed group dance numbers and being good at wearing ball gowns. At twelve, I both craved the approval of others and was delusional with preteen hormones. I applied for the pageant, obviously.

I do not remember specifics about the application process as I have buried them deep within the shame part of my brain. I'm guessing it required a headshot as my mom recently cursed me with a stack of pageant-era photos she found in the basement, glossy eight-by-tens of me close-mouthed smiling with braces and looking moody on our family's front porch. I'm assuming I attached some sort of "résumé" consisting of my GPA, extracurricular activities, favorite color, and other innocuous things about my twelve-year-old self. There may have been an essay portion. If there was, I'm sure I wrote something sad, desperate, and pseudo-inspirational, like, *My name is Mia, and sometimes I hope I'll become famous overnight so I don't have to turn in my social studies homework in the morning. If you accept me into this pageant, it would mean the world to me as it would finally give me something to talk to my crush Matt S. about. Thank you and, also, you're welcome!*

I know, with certainty, it cost $400 to submit an application. (Did you know the average US college application costs about $50?) I was twelve and had no money. My parents were rich with unconditional love.

My application for the pageant was accepted, and I was named a "regional finalist" or "county finalist" or some other meaningless title the pageant coordinators chose to best convey, "This mess of acne and braces hereby referred to as 'preteen girl' somehow convinced her parents to pay hundreds of dollars so she could stomp around in a fancy dress and have adult strangers decide if she stomps the prettiest." I wouldn't be surprised if everyone who applied for the pageant and paid $400 was named a "finalist."

I don't know if I will ever understand why my parents let me do it. "Disposable income" was not really a thing that existed in my family of six. This isn't to say I felt deprived of fun little treats growing up. My mom, sister, and I would raid the Kohl's clearance rack before every school year. Every once in a while, my parents would take all four of us kids through the Dairy Queen drive-through and we'd all shout "Dilly Bar" or "StarKiss" from the back seat. This is to say, however, that I still feel a sense of guilt when I peruse regular-priced racks. Also, I had no idea Blizzards were an option on the Dairy Queen menu until well into high school.

Maybe my parents thought letting me do this pageant would shut me up about thinking I deserved my own Disney Channel show. (It didn't.) More likely, they were overcome by the aforementioned unconditional love and worn down by the hyperdramatics of my preteen self. Regardless, they have yet another humiliating thing to hold over my head should I ever threaten to put them in a home.

My preparation for the pageant was minimal. My mom took me to the juniors' clothing store Maurice's—most of my coming-of-age moments happened in juniors' clothing stores—and I picked out the twenty dollar-est dress for the "formal wear" portion of the competition. I may have Naired my entire body. I did not pluck my eyebrows.

The pageant took place the summer before my eighth-grade year, in a hotel in the middle of Wisconsin. Girls from across the state came in their department store finest to parade around a conference room and say their name nervously into a microphone. My entire family and my best friend, Sami, came to the competition, all seven of us staying in one hotel room together. I'm sure I started anxiety sweating the moment I walked into pre-pageant prep meetings with my extremely suburban entourage.

In trying to avoid being associated with my family even a little bit, I remember sitting with a fellow competitor named Jenna. She had blond hair curled into perfect ringlets and looked like a tween who'd be cast as an extra in a Lip Smacker commercial. She was a girl who would usually be too cool to talk to me, but here in this carpeted hotel ballroom, we were equals.

"Ohmigahd are you really not wearing foundation?!" she asked me at one point, staring closely at my face. I told her no as it was against competition rules to wear any noticeable makeup. Ball gowns, heels, and media training for preteens? Good, fine, very normal. A detectable smoky eye or tinted lip? That's where the pageant organizers drew the line. The mindfuck that is "natural beauty" entered my vocabulary around this time.

During one of the first pre-pageant prep meetings, the contestants and our parents were greeted by the woman who ran the show. Her hair was big (teased with the hopes of preteen girls), and she had a slight southern accent I'm still not convinced was real. She is exactly who you picture when I say "pageant head mistress." She gave us a rundown of the next couple days and playfully assured the parents that when they left the room, she would not be "taking the girls to Denny's." Though I don't have kids, I'm guessing a bad way to reassure parents is to say, "I won't kidnap your kids, promise!" However, "taking the girls to Denny's" is now the euphemism I use whenever I cook eggs topless.

Pageant Head Mistress also repeatedly mentioned how the pageant after-party would only have cake and punch, "NO SHRIMP COCKTAIL." She was adamant the post-pageant party would include absolutely zero shrimp cocktail. I'm sure this was a deal breaker for the highfalutin crowd definitely in attendance at this suburban Wisconsin preteen beauty pageant.

Once the parents left, the pageant prep meetings were kind of like a wedding rehearsal: the pageant coordinators told us who needed to go where and when to stand. They told us when to smile (always) and how the show would run (poorly). We were taught choreography to the show's opening number, a group dance to "Jump Jump" by Aaron Carter. I can probably still do the choreo, and I'm guessing you could too as we basically just did whatever the lyrics said to do. When Aaron Carter said "JUMP," we jumped. When Aaron Carter said "to the left, to the right," we pointed stage left and then stage right.

After a handful of prep meetings, the actual pageant began. Unlike contestants who'd hired coaches or the television toddlers who you may have seen in tiaras, most of my experience with pageants involved watching Miss America on TV or seeing the Kirsten Dunst vehicle *Drop Dead Gorgeous* a little too young. I assumed a pageant was one singular event where we, the contestants, confidently walked around onstage in sporty outfits, casual outfits, and then evening gowns. (What kind of evening did I anticipate having at twelve that required a gown? Who knows, but it certainly required matching heels as well!) I thought there would be a lot more waving elegantly. I thought there would be significantly more posing. I thought I'd get to answer questions live onstage like "In thirty seconds or less, how would you solve gender inequality?" and "Is ISIS really that bad?" The actual pageant was only kind of like that.

Most of the judged events took place prior to the big show that was open to the public. (Who was this public desperate to attend a preteen beauty pageant? TV agents? Modeling scouts? Perverts and yet more perverts?) There were three portions in which all girls were required to compete: the opening number, formal wear, and interview. The opening number—the choreographed dance to Aaron Carter—was the only judged event that took place during the actual "show." The show, which would be attended by parents, the public, and perverts alike, was the final pageant event, where winners would be announced and awards given out.

Over the next day or so, contestant interviews were conducted. We were told to wear business-appropriate attire for the interviews, which involved us sitting one-on-one with one of the pageant judges. I wish they would have made us develop a backstory to go along with our interview wear, going into detail about what kind of business I, a twelve-year-old girl who'd barely left the state of Wisconsin, intended to conduct in an ill-fitting power suit. I donned a cream blazer and a matching skirt I'd bought with my mom at, I'm assuming, Sears. While shopping for the outfit, we probably left my dad and brothers to stare at the dishwashers or Cheetos—Sears truly had *everything*. I'm guessing I cried in the dressing room.

On interview day, I wore a powder blue, mock turtleneck sleeveless top under my blazer. (It should be illegal for a garment to require that many descriptors. I will give you a moment to process.) I know I complained more than once about the blazer's shoulder pads, which I worried made me look old but not in a cool way. Once dressed, I slipped on my half-inch cream pumps, likely the first time I'd worn heels. If you need to wear high heels for the first time, it's best to do it while twelve years old and walking down a carpeted hotel hallway to a pageant interview. It really amplifies just how stupid everything is all the time.

The sight of a hundred or so preteen girls in business wear must be like a renaissance painting come to life. You learn quickly whose parents made them wear pantyhose (and called them as such—much different than "tights" or "nylons"). You see whose mom had taught them to shave their legs, some the morning of the interview. You see which girls had parents with money based on who matched their braces' bands to their outfit, their shoes to their shirt, their sweaty foreheads to their sweaty feet. You see who, at twelve or thirteen, already had more confidence than you will ever be able to muster as an adult person.

The interviews were conducted in a speed-dating style. The handful of judges sat at separate circle tables around a hotel conference room, waiting with clipboards and coffee breath for a new round of girls to file in. I only remember speaking with one judge. I may have spoken to more and blacked out completely, but I know for certain I was interviewed by one kind woman with strong grandma vibes. (She could have been in her late thirties, but my child brain registered her as "grandma.") We may have shaken hands. I likely stumbled when saying my own name, like it wasn't something I'd carried with me my whole life but a surprise the Pageant Head Mistress had thrown at me moments before I walked into the interview room and I'd just barely managed to catch. The interview couldn't have lasted more than five minutes, ten tops. There were over a hundred girls competing and no more than five or six judges. I doubt they kept the judges in the conference room for more than an hour and a half. Any more would certainly be illegal for everyone involved.

The only question I remember being asked in my interview was, "What is your favorite book?" A softball. A gimme. Truly an easy and inconsequential question. Sometimes I wonder if my pageant score would have been different had I answered with a different book. Was *Running Out of Time* by Margaret Peterson Haddix the butterfly that set off my pageant fate?

If you aren't familiar, *Running Out of Time* is a YA novel from the mid-'90s about a thirteen-year-old girl who lives in the 1840s . . . or so she thinks. Through a diphtheria outbreak, she learns the year is actually 1996 and everyone in this village is part of some social experiment/tourist attraction. If that sounds like an M. Night Shyamalan–level twist, that's probably because you saw *The Village*, the 2004 Joaquin Phoenix vehicle that has undeniable similarities to Haddix's story. What I'm saying is I blame any and all of my pageant-related problems on M. Night Shyamalan.

I like to imagine how the pageant judge would have reacted had I said my favorite book was the Bible or *A Clockwork Orange* or *There's a Wocket in My Pocket!* What if twelve-year-old me had looked this pageant judge in the eyes and said, "My favorite book is all the softcovers because those taste the best"? I wonder if that would've gone over equally as well as me talking about a book that I hadn't read since fourth grade.

The judged formal wear portion of the pageant happened next. While we would be wearing our formal wear during the actual show, we would be scored beforehand. I'm guessing the judges wanted to figure out their winners way before the night of the public show. Or they just liked the idea of making a bunch of preteens feel uncomfortable in floor-length dresses as many times as possible. The formal wear event went like this: The pageant emcee would announce each contestant with an index card she'd gotten beforehand. The card would have our name, where we were from, and an interesting fact like our hobbies or what we wanted to be when we grew up. When we heard our name, we'd walk out onto the stage, accompanied by a male.

The male escort (LOL) could be a dad, a younger brother, an estranged uncle, a neighbor with poor discretion, pretty much anyone as long as he was male. The pageant organizers were adamant that the escort *must* be male, as a female escort (LOL x 2) would "pull focus." We, the preteen contestants with a literal number pinned to our dresses, had to be the hottest or at least only-est female in view! If there was more than one woman on stage, how would the judges know who was the preteen contestant and who was the escort? Which person should they be judging, the twelve-year-old in heels or the fully adult woman in comfortable flats? There would be no way to tell!

If a contestant didn't have a male to escort her during the formal wear portion, one would be provided. My dad was supposed to escort me during the formal wear event, him in a tuxedo and me in a dress that managed to incorporate both black lace and gold lamé.

Unfortunately, shortly before the judged formal wear event, my dad was unable to find his dress pants. We frantically checked the hotel closet, the hallway, the front desk, the car, but alas, my dad's pants were gone. (We later found out they'd fallen off the hanger at home.) By the grace of the pants-stealing gods, my dad had been spared the humiliation of having video footage of him escorting me, his twelve-year-old daughter, onstage while "*untz untz untz*" music throbbed in the background and an emcee butchered my last name.

And yes, we *did* get a DVD recording of the pageant for me to watch over and over again, like a former high school football player reliving his glory days or an adult woman retraumatizing herself with middle school memories. This DVD is how I know that during the formal wear portion of the public pageant I was introduced as such:

Contestant number 47: Amelia Mer-sah . . . Mer-kay-dough! Amelia is escorted by her friend, Dale . . .

After I told the pageant organizers "my dad forgot his pants," I was assigned someone else's dad to be my escort. In the hierarchy of escort appropriateness, Stranger Dad with Pants usurps Actual Dad Without Pants. Mom or Woman of Any Kind is nowhere in that hierarchy.

Dale wore a suit, had a reddish mustache, and looked no more comfortable to be walking arm-in-arm with a female minor than I looked to be walking arm-in-arm with a man I'd just met. Being introduced as "friends" in front of a crowd of strangers, his family, and my family was a new layer of hell we'd unlocked together.

Now, before you get too intimidated by the fact that you may be reading something written by the reigning 2003 National American Miss Pre-teen Wisconsin, let me tell you: I did not win.

Before you wonder, "Okay, but surely you made Top 15, given your natural introversion and poor, twelve-year-old interpersonal skills," let me go on record and say: I did not make Top 15.

Before you think, "Sure, fine. No big deal. Top 15 out of one hundred plus girls doesn't exactly put the odds in your favor. But you had to have won Most Photogenic, a portion of the competition your parents paid an extra $50 for you to enter, using more photos Dad took of you leaning against a tree and slouching on the broken swing set in the backyard . . . right?" Let me stop you right now: I did not even get Top 5 Most Photogenic.

Before the life leaves your eyes and hope leaves your heart entirely, begging, "What about Most Spirited? Miss Personality? Best Volunteer Service? Most Promise as a Model? Best Résumé? Most Tickets Sold, given to the girl who sold the most tickets for the pageant? Most Recommendations, given to the girl who referred the most other girls to participate in the pageant? BEST THANK YOU NOTE TO A SPONSOR???" I need to tell you: (1) Yes, those were all actual awards given out and (2) the only prize I won was a participation trophy. I quite literally won nothing. It's fine, I'm over it, but I still should have gotten at least fourth most photogenic.

You may wonder why I recount this story at all, why I choose to relive this days-long marathon in prepubescent embarrassment, why for the love of God my parents let me do this. While yes, I now have both memories and video footage of me dancing in jean shorts to Aaron Carter, me attempting to walk in heels looking like Bambi on ice, me smiling while linking arms with a dad I'd just met, and me crying on stage after realizing I would not be 2003 National American Miss Pre-teen Wisconsin, I have only now come to realize that I am not what is most embarrassing here.

I am no longer embarrassed for myself, a child with dreams of saying, "You're watching Disney Channel" while doing the cool, CGI wand thing. I am certainly not embarrassed for the girl who won this pageant and then went on to win more pageants, competing well into her late teens. (I am only a little embarrassed to admit that I still remember her full name and have googled her as recently as this morning. FOR RESEARCH PURPOSES ONLY, obviously.)

I do feel full secondhand embarrassment for the adults running the event. The grown people organizing, hosting, judging, and ultimately profiting from preteens in Kohl's clearance-wear were by far the most hilarious and humiliating part of the spectacle. There was the aforementioned Pageant Head Mistress Supreme, likely somewhere still screaming about NO SHRIMP COCKTAIL. There was one of the competition judges (different from the woman who'd interviewed me) who was a literal Navy vet with a bachelor's degree in aeronautical science. So if you're keeping track, his résumé goes: Pilot, Veteran, Preteen Pageant Judge. Take some time to try to connect those dots however you see fit.

Then there was the pageant host, the woman in, I'm guessing, her early thirties who emceed the public pageant show. A woman who I can only assume is the product of "always the runner-up, never the pageant queen," which I say with only partial judgment because at least she likely got more than a participation trophy. (Again, not bitter, but I'd still like to know if even one of my peers voted me "Miss Personality.")

The pageant host was confident with a microphone, knew how to work a crowd, and had a real gravitas when welcoming everyone to the "2003 Minnesota National American Miss Pageant!" We were in Wisconsin.

After the Top 15 were announced, all of the pageant contestants were made to come back on stage. We stood on risers, in numerical order, holding our participation trophies. We tried not to sob as we stared at the back of the heads of the fifteen girls who'd be moving on in the pageant. We definitely sobbed a bunch.

It was during this moment—after ninety-plus girls just found out they lost the pageant they'd been competing in for the last few days—the pageant host chose to perform a song. She, dressed in a dark, strappy gown, hair slicked into a low bun, took the cordless microphone, and the intro to "Wind Beneath My Wings" began.

She, the adult female pageant host, proceeded to spend the next five entire minutes serenading the audience and the Top 15 contestants. She half-consolingly sang to the risers full of pre-teen girls who just found out they lost the competition. *You're everything I wish I could be*, she crooned directly to a dead-eyed girl in a bejeweled A-line dress who refused to so much as smile while this adult stranger sang at her. *I could fly hiiiiigher than an eagle*, she belted, adding three extra syllables to the word "eagle." *'Cause you are the wind beneath my wings*, she finished while touching the shoulder of a Top 15 girl.

I and the other ninety-some losers were finally able to leave the risers. We sat backstage for the duration of the pageant, watching from offstage as the remaining contestants took a second lap around the stage. We sat in the rows of hotel conference room chairs reserved for this moment specifically. Some of us slouching and sobbing, most of us shoeless, all of us reverting to our natural preteen form.

Afterward, my family, my friend Sami, and I all went to the post-pageant party. There was, as promised, no shrimp cocktail.

HOLLYWOOD AND MEDIA REPRESENTATION PRESENTS: HOW WOMEN AGE

Prebirth (A Literal Fetus)

This is when a female has the most power. She is not born yet and is therefore worth protecting and valuing. An unborn female can become anything: a Daughter, a Wife, a Mother, anything!

FAMOUS PREBIRTH WOMEN: Katherine Heigl's baby bump in *Knocked Up*; Blue Ivy when she was still inside of Beyoncé; whichever daughter Demi Moore was pregnant with when she did that naked *Vanity Fair* cover

Baby (Three to Twenty-Four Months Old)

In movies, babies of every gender are either not born yet or already a few months old. There is no such thing as a newborn. You will know the baby is female because she wears pink outfits, has bows in her hair, says "Sorry" before she cries, and gets paid less than her male baby double.

FAMOUS BABY WOMEN: the baby in *American Sniper*; Mary-Kate and Ashley on *Full House*, Seasons 1–3; Baby Jessica who fell in the well

Toddler (Two to Five Years Old)

The only female toddlers that exist are unusual, cute, dead, or some combination of the three. Try to think of a female toddler who was just normal and boring. You can't! It's because there have never been any. Even if you think you remember a time you saw one, you probably just saw a doll or a dog walking on its hind legs and got confused.

FAMOUS TODDLER WOMEN: Mary-Kate and Ashley on *Full House*, Seasons 4–7; JonBenét Ramsey; Honey Boo Boo

Precocious Kid Detective
(Six to Nine Years Old)

There is a brief time in a female's life where she can have a Male Job. It's when she's old enough to ride a bike but not quite old enough to understand first-degree murder.

FAMOUS KID DETECTIVES: Harriet the Spy, Penny from *Inspector Gadget*, Mary-Kate and Ashley in their *Adventures of Mary-Kate and Ashley* series

Period (Ten to Thirteen Years Old)

When a Daughter gets her period in secret, she becomes a woman. More specifically, she becomes a woman who could either become a Wife or a Mother. If she gets her period in public, she becomes a Cautionary Tale.

FAMOUS PERIOD WOMEN: Margaret from *Are You There God? It's Me, Margaret*; Anna Chlumsky's character in *My Girl*; Carrie

Virgin (Fourteen to Seventeen Years Old)

Eventually, people will start wanting to have sex with the female. If that female is a Daughter, this is rather unsavory. No one wants to imagine their Daughter having sex!!! That is gross and awful in a way you can't quite put your finger in, I mean, on.

FAMOUS VIRGIN WOMEN: the Virgin Mary; Disney Princesses (except Jasmine; she definitely fucks); pre-*1989*-era Taylor Swift

Whore (Eighteen Years Old and Older)

In some instances, the female wants to have sex with other people. This is absolutely disgusting, unspeakable, and should be ignored entirely. (Unless you're in a private browser window.)

FAMOUS WHORES: Mary Magdalene; me; you; any female who says things like "My body, my choice" or wears skirts and lipstick or uses birth control and isn't married or lives with a guy or likes girls or dances to Cardi B; Taylor Swift but only in that one horny song; Marilyn Monroe

Hot Mom (Nineteen to Twenty-Four Years Old)

The ultimate dream for every female is to one day become a Hot Mom! Hot Moms have it ALL: great kids, loving husband, work at home, wine, being home all day, gossip with the gals, wine, underdeveloped backstory, big hair, no wants or needs that exist independently of her role as a Mom or Wife, and did I mention wine? Let's hear it for all the Hot Moms!

FAMOUS HOT MOMS: Connie Britton in the commercials for *Friday Night Lights*; all the women in diaper commercials; how your dad remembers Christie Brinkley

Regular Mom
(Twenty-Five to Thirty-Five Years Old)

She's just a Hot Mom except a little more approachable. In other words, she swears sometimes and is probably portrayed by Leslie Mann (who is still Hot in an approachable way).

FAMOUS REGULAR MOMS: Leslie Mann in *Knocked Up*; Leslie Mann in *Neighbors*; Leslie Mann in *This Is 40*; oh wait, that was Rose Byrne in *Neighbors*—which is like Leslie Mann but Australian

Dead Mom (Any Age)

Every Mom dreams of the day when she will become a Dead Mom. Dead Moms are pious. Dead Moms are revered. Dead Moms are used as motivation for male characters' revenge stories and thought of fondly in a flashback where you only see her legs and the bottom half of an apron. Regardless of the age at which she died, all Dead Moms will be portrayed in pictures/flashbacks by a twentysomething Jennifer Lawrence.

FAMOUS DEAD MOMS: Bambi's mom; Danny Tanner's wife from *Full House*; the Joker's Mom (We don't see her but we can just assume they had a tough relationship. Even serial killers deserve some sympathy! Unless they're women. Then they were probably just on their Period.)

Grandma
(Thirty-Nine to Forty-Five Years Old)

At the seasoned old age of thirty-nine, a female becomes a Grandma. Even if she doesn't have children, let alone grandchildren, she is, in the eyes of Hollywood, a Grandma. Grandmas are similar to Moms except we know even less about their likes, interests, and sexual activity.

FAMOUS GRANDMAS: Danny Tanner's Dead Wife in *Fuller House* (Dead Grandmas still count as just Grandmas); Sofía Vergara in *Modern Family* (Step-Grandma Representation win!!!); Mrs. Claus (she's actually only forty-one!)

Statue in the Background of a Park Scene
(Age Forty-Five Plus)

There are so many opportunities for women over the age of forty-five in Hollywood. They can truly be anything: extras in TV shows; extras in osteoporosis commercials; extras in a music video where they're sexualized but it's kinda supposed to be funny; anything! Women forty-five and older are crucial to creating a realistic environment in a movie . . . because they are literally part of the background environment in a movie.

FAMOUS WOMEN WHO WERE STATUES IN THE BACKGROUND OF A PARK SCENE: The "Feed the Birds" lady from *Mary Poppins* (you thought she was real but she was played by a gargoyle come to life); the Statue of Liberty; whoever your mom's favorite actress is

Exceptions

These women may appear anywhere, at any time, for any reason, regardless of age:

1. Helen Mirren

2. Betty White

3. Downton Abbey

4. Old pictures of Marilyn Monroe

5. Beyoncé

6. Betty Boop

7. I'm being told "Downton Abbey" isn't
   a person, but you get what I mean
   (what I mean is that if she's British, it's okay)

8. Jessica Rabbit

Alternative Women

The above almost exclusively applies to white and white-passing females. (Beyoncé is the only exception on account of her being Beyoncé.) Because there isn't a big enough sample size for actors of color, women who are not white should follow these basic rules of thumb:

- Asian women go from young, fuckable porcelain dolls to old, wizened apple cores. There is no in-between.

- Latinx women age similarly. However, as a child, they can be the "why not both" tortilla girl. As an adult, they will be described as "spicy" or "hot" or some other word on a Cholula bottle. If they are not hot, then they are "abuela."

- Black women's age is only discussed in terms of surprise (e.g., Lisa Bonet is *how old*??!?!!??!).

- All nonwhite women may play a housekeeper, nurse, maid, etc., at any age! Wow! Did you see when we said "nurse"? We love women of color in STEM but mostly when they are YOUNG and HOT!

The above specifications apply exclusively to women who are conventionally hot, straight, cis, able-bodied, medium to long hair, at least middle class, no mental health problems (unless it's daddy issues!), have big boobs that are real, are hairless, have a big butt if that's still popular, and can eat a whole pizza and still be so thin. If the woman falls into any other category, ugh okay that's fine we guess, but it must only be for comedy.

BATH & BODY WORKS IS THE SUBURBAN NONSENSE I CRAVE

Today, I am here because I "need" candles. This will be the first of many lies I tell myself on this trip.

There is no scenario in which scented candles are a necessity for anyone. Are you performing a séance that only summons demons with a realistic sugar cookie scent? Do you only work by cherry blossom candlelight? Or are you just committed to perpetuating the lie that your home naturally smells like fruity ocean water despite living in a landlocked state and having to google "bergamot orange real fruit or just candle smell"? No one "needs" candles, but if you're gonna come with me on this journey, leave your bullshit attitude about my priorities on that mall bench next to all the disillusioned dads.

This Bath & Body Works is located in a mall next to a Target and a Starbucks. I'm a selfie-stick kiosk away from fully awakening my Inner Soccer Mom. As I cross the store's threshold, I am harassed by twenty different sugary scents and a woman doling out shopping bags with a T-shirt cannon. The general vibe of Bath & Body Works is "house of funky aunt who always has cake for some reason and keeps reminding you your ovaries have an expiration date." The store smells like I'm being hugged by every grandmother in America, every nana with a cup of cocoa, every mee-maw with a scalding hot apple strudel. And if you took that last one as a euphemism: welcome. Everything you see and smell at The Works is a euphemism. I'll look you dead in the eyes while buying a hand lotion labeled "sensual."

I begin my ritual of huffing anything with a wick within arm's reach. This is both an effective smell test method as well as an upper-body workout because their candles weigh as much as a newborn. You think a baby smells nice? Try going nose-deep into a three-wick Mahogany Teakwood. If you didn't come to get high on a Warm Apple Pie votive while douching yourself with a clearance foaming soap, what are you even doing here?

I hear a woman yell, "Ooooh, their seasonal scents are out!" The war cry of my people. There's a fragrance called Flannel. It's a cute, wintery smell that's code for, "We took the deodorant-laden armpits of your ex-boyfriend's T-shirt and infused them with hope, pining, and actual pine. Basically, you're about to drop $22.50 on a candle that'll make you sad and horny at the same time."

There is a tester version of everything. Their goal is to make you sample so many lotions, your hands will be too moisturized to grip the door handle and you can't leave. I know women who have spent their entire twenties in a Bath & Body Works. I choose to pay my respects to the twelve hundred different body mists with a hearty spritz of each one. My goal is to leave this store smelling like a baked good you want to hump.

Like any good trip, I black out and end up with $75 worth of soap cradled in my arms. Some may say that's excessive, but only if you have a healthy understanding of fiscal responsibility. Before you get too judgmental, I do have a coupon. I'm on their mailing list because the subject lines of their email deals are the kind of passive-aggression I am here for. My inbox is littered with messages like "Seriously. Last chance for $10 body mist" and "We have your family. Buy our foot cream."

I leave with three more coupons than I came with because Bath & Body Works takes a human centipede approach to marketing. They feed you coupons so you shit out money and buy sugar scrubs to get more coupons, so you shit out more money for more sugar scrubs. I plan to repeat this cycle until I die or my body just becomes a skin tube of shower gel. I'm honestly not sure which will come first.

As I leave, I try not to become distracted by a candle display I'm convinced only revealed itself as I was attempting to exit. I dodge through a gauntlet of cookie-scented air fresheners for a car. You know, where every human bakes all their cookies. After donkey-kicking through a thick haze of perfume and room spray, I finally find myself on the outside of the store. I get to my car and realize I forgot to buy candles. I will "need" to come back tomorrow.

ITEMS OF CLOTHING, DEFINED

Pants

Pants are what you wear on your lower half. They exist only as an indicator of where you are currently located. Pants on? Outside, in the world. Pants off? At your home. Pants half on and half off? Probably, hopefully, in a bathroom. There are multiple subcategories of Pants, including:

- **JEANS:** Once made of stiff, immovable denim, Jeans are now becoming stretchier and more comfortable. Did you know long, long ago, people used to come home after a long day of work, kick back, relax, and put on Jeans?! Imagine feeling relaxed in a pair of Jeans.

- **SWEATPANTS:** Sweatpants are one of the few items of clothing that live up to their name. They are called "Sweatpants" because they are Pants and you don't sweat or do any physical activity in them.

- **SHORTS:** These are summertime Pants that range in length from Capris to Huh, I Didn't Know They Made Underwear out of Corduroy.

- **LEGGINGS/YOGA PANTS/ATHLEISURE:** Wish your Sweatpants showed more of your camel toe? Try Leggings!

- **SKIRT**: A Skirt is Pants that ripped away from the crotch down each leg. That is the only reason a Skirt would exist. No one would have created them otherwise. The only intentionally made Skirt is a Poodle Skirt. It is a Skirt made for Poodles, by Poodles.

Shirt

Shirts, which are essentially Opposite Pants, are categorized by sleeve length.

- **T-SHIRT**: This is called that because it looks like the letter "T."

- **LONG-SLEEVE TEE**: This is like a capital "T-shirt," in the sense that it looks like the letter "T" received capital punishment that made its top bar get stretched out in opposite directions by horses.

- **TANK TOP**: This is what you wear when you want everyone to know you have biceps.

- **HALTER TOP**: This is what you wear when you want everyone to know you have shoulders.

- **SPAGHETTI-STRAP TANK TOP**: This is what you wear when you want everyone to know you have spaghetti.

- **BANDEAU TOP**: This is just a headband that got lost.

You can wear a Shirt on its own or in layers. One Shirt is perfectly acceptable. However, two Shirts can signal a lot about your identity. It can say you're someone who knows how to use a monkey wrench (a white tee and a flannel) or you're someone who knows how to use an acoustic guitar (a band tee and a flannel) or you're someone who doesn't understand how Shirts work at all (a flannel and another flannel).

Sweatshirt

A Sweatshirt, sometimes called a "Hoodie," is what straight girls wear to signal that they have a boyfriend. You'll know because they will tell you that this is their boyfriend's Hoodie and ugh it's *so comfy* and smells like him (bad).

Jacket

A Jacket is what cool people wear to signify their coolness. It is solely a prop for them to take off, swing over one shoulder, holding on to the collar using one finger, and say, "You new here?"

Tie

This is like a pull string for businesspeople. If you pull the Tie, the business person will say things like "Our fourth-quarter earnings are looking good!" and "Synergy!" and "What the hell, stop it, did Janine let you in here?"

Dress

A Dress is what happens when a trash bag goes to fashion design school or a potato sack sees *The Devil Wears Prada* once. It is somehow tight and loose, constricting yet revealing, slutty yet matronly all at the same time. There are different types of Dresses for different types of occasions:

- **COCKTAIL DRESS**: Any Dress you've spilled wine on.

- **SUMMER DRESS**: A Dress you wear when you want people to think you fuck in a meadow.

- **LITTLE BLACK DRESS**: A Dress you wear when you want people to think you fuck in a rom-com way.

- **EVENING GOWN**: A Dress you wear when you want people to think you fuck in a sophisticated way. Pinkies up!

Overalls

Always wished you could feel like your shirt and pants were both giving you a wedgie at the same time? Overalls are for you!

Romper

Love getting completely naked to pee in public bathrooms? Try a Romper!

Socks

Socks are that feeling you get at 2 a.m. when you're trying to fall asleep and suddenly you are simultaneously so hot and so cold. They are knitted prisons, and nobody knows why they exist.

Tights/Nylons

See "Socks" but worse.

Hat

This is what you wear instead of developing a personality.

Scarves

Similar to a Hat, a Scarf is a substitute for a female character's backstory in a movie. If the character layers enough Scarves, she eventually becomes a love interest.

Belt

This is a Scarf you put in time-out. It has been bad and now it is being punished by having to keep your butt from falling out of your Pants.

Gloves/Mittens

Gloves are like a pair of fabric skin for your hands. There is a Glove or Mitten for every occasion!

- **WINTER GLOVES:** Fuzzy, felt hand skin for the winter!

- **BASEBALL MITT:** Tough, leather big hand for sport!

- **OVEN MITT:** Thick, round hand protector for not catching fire!

- **WHITE GLOVES (SHORT):** If your white gloves stop at your wrist, abracadabra! You're a magician!

- **WHITE GLOVES (LONG):** If your white gloves extend up your forearm, ooh, la la! You're a debutante!

- **WHITE GLOVE (WHOLE BODY):** Congratulations! You're the Hamburger Helper mascot!

Shoes

Shoes are what complete an outfit. They are also the only part of our clothes we find acceptable to touch the nasty, bad, outside ground. Some people pay upward of $100 for Shoes, a thing you press your entire body weight into and sometimes touches shit that's not even yours. Shoes can serve as a signature character trait for people of every gender! (Sneaker Guy, High Heel Girl, Tap Dancer, WikiFeet User.) They are also what you put on to make your dog feel excited and then sad and lonely.

Underwear

This is the item of clothing you tell all your worst secrets to.

Bra

This is what you take off to finally feel free.

DOES THIS COUNT AS EXERCISE?

I drink thirty-two ounces of water by noon. Hydration, I hear, is important if you're going to work out. In the same amount of time, I have gotten up to pee an estimated forty times. Does this count as exercise?

I drive to the gym. When I get there, I immediately get anxious diarrhea. I spend about as much time in the bathroom as I would have on the treadmill. Does that count as exercise?

Does it count as exercise if I put on yoga pants to vacuum? What about if I also wear yoga pants while washing dishes? Does the act of wearing yoga pants dub anything I do yoga? If it helps, I do say "Namaste" constantly and with no discretion when I wear them.

Once, I got a massage—this I know is *not* an exercise and if it is, something has gone awry—and the masseuse asked what I do to work out. She asked so she would know what muscles to focus on. I answered like she had any actual stake in my fitness regimen. "Uh, I take my dog on walks," I panicked, leaving out the part where my dog often lies down on the first patch of grass she sees and refuses to get up. (To be fair, it is her punishment for me, a human, for my kind having bred her kind for cuteness and not lung capacity.) "Also, I do Pilates sometimes." I haven't done anything remotely resembling Pilates since 2009. I sweat when I lie. So, that makes this whole conversation exercise, right?

Does hovering over a public toilet count as a squat? Did I work out my glutes if I held in a fart for a long time? Does getting up the nerve to ask the barista for the bathroom code burn any calories?

I've made it through multiple conversations where people, apropos of nothing, tell me about an Asian friend they have or an Asian coworker they know or an Asian person they saw one time at, wow would you believe it, an Asian restaurant. I never scream or even punch them a little. Showing that kind of restraint has *got* to be exercise.

I take a nap in a sports bra and wake up in a cold sweat because I had a stress dream about high school. I'm twenty-nine. Have I just done an exercise?

I feel a sense of physical exhaustion whenever a man tries to get me to watch *Lord of the Rings*. Do you think that's because both watching the movie and having that conversation are forms of exercise?

My heart rate definitely increases every time I think about the scene where Devon Sawa's Casper turns from cartoon ghost into a human teen boy. Does that make it exercise?

I get a run in my tights. Have I just done leg day?

It would definitely count as exercise if someone would make a Map My Run but for my daily mental run through every bad thing I've said in the past fifteen years.

As someone who took actual gymnastics as a child, I can tell you that mental gymnastics requires just as much flexibility and adults yelling at you to TRY HARDER and STOP CRYING ABOUT THE BALANCE BEAM.

At the end of the day, I lie in bed trying to relax every part of my dense, anxiety ball of a body for once in my life. How do I hold this much tension in my forehead and cheeks?! For the first time all day, my limbs are loose, my shoulders are at ease, and my brain's only running thought is RELAX RELAX FOR THE LOVE OF GOD RELAX. While this is not exercise, it could maybe pass as meditation . . . which, if you think about it, is a kind of mental workout in itself. Perhaps I have done an exercise after all.

Part 4

ON BEING Horny AND IN ♡ Love ♡

AND SOMETIMES EVEN BOTH

These are stories on dating, relationships, fucking, not fucking, cultural sexualization, and, more often, all of those things happening at once. They're about what's expected of each party in a heterosexual relationship, how relationships are expected to be heterosexual, how I don't understand how everyone of every orientation isn't endlessly and outwardly horny for Michael B. Jordan.

They're stories about my misinterpretations of sex, my extremely correct interpretations of sex, and things that are sexual even if they are not meant to be.

These are stories that you can skip if you are my parents.

ALL THE THINGS
I THOUGHT SEX WAS

I never got the "sex talk" from my parents. If I did, I must have *Eternal Sunshine*-ed it out of my brain entirely. Long before sex was a thing I thought about doing, I had a mental catalog of what sex entailed based on things I learned from friends, movies, and the internet. Much to my prepubescent chagrin, that mental catalog was both incomplete and had little to no credibility. In attempts to cite my sources, here are all the things I presumed sex to be.

Sex has something to do with your fingers.

I first got the sex talk from a classmate in third grade who demonstrated the act using her hands. "This is what kissing is," she said, touching the tips of her index fingers together. "This is what sex is," she said, holding them parallel and pointing opposite directions, rubbing her fingers back and forth, moving each fingertip down to the base of the opposite finger, her expression unchanging.

I told my parents when I got home from school that day, probably recounting it in the same way I talked about our daily lesson in language arts or social studies. *Today, we practiced our times tables, and Catherine P. said that sex is when people kiss privates.* In other words, I thought sex was 69ing. I was never assigned a seat next to Catherine P. again.

Sperm is sexual but in a gross way.

By the time I reached fifth grade, I knew that sex involved being naked and did not necessarily require mouth-to-peen/vageen contact. (Thanks for nothing, Catherine P.) I was pretty sure it had something to do with vaginas and penises and those things feeling good somehow, but the mechanics of it all were still beyond me.

During a springtime class picnic—if nothing else, I hope you come away from this knowing that midwestern elementary schools are exactly as quaint and heteronormative as you assume—I sat with a group of girls and ate sandwiches. A glob of mayonnaise dripped out of one girl's sandwich and fell onto the sidewalk. Everyone started giggling, talking about how gross it was.

I laughed along like *Ew look at that nasty sidewalk mayo yucky ha ha I totally get why we're laughing like this.* One of the girls turned to me and said, "You know what that looks like, right?" I nodded, unconvincingly. My friend Sami, the one who would years later witness me losing the National American Miss Preteen Wisconsin title, leaned over to me and whispered, "It looks like sperm." I did not know what sperm was, let alone what it looked like. However, I thought if it looked anything like the mayonnaise on a sidewalk—it, scientifically, should not—I knew it was disgusting.

Sex is when girls do body rolls while dancing.

Like most pre-internet ten-year-olds, I learned a lot about sex from watching *Coyote Ugly* and *Center Stage* back-to-back during a sleepover. For me, the sleepover occurred at Brittany S.'s house. Yes, this is the same Brittany S. whose coveted cool girl top led to my mom calling out my armpit hair in the dressing room at Fashion Bug (see page 119). In hindsight, a surprising number of my coming-of-age moments feature Brittany S., someone who I'm sure cannot remember how to spell my last name.

Getting invited to a sleepover at Brittany S.'s gave me imposter syndrome. *No way* was I cool enough to have a sleepover at Brittany S.'s, whose parents let her have her own phone in her bedroom. Yeah, *right*, I'd be allowed to hang out in my cartoon frog–patterned Kohl's pajamas alongside Kristin A., who wore black plastic choker necklaces every day, and Jamie Z., who'd had full-on boobs since, like, third grade. Being at a sleepover with girls I thought far cooler than me was both my dream heaven and personal anxiety hell.

After gossiping (!) and calling boys (!!) on the phone (!!!), Brittany said we should watch *Coyote Ugly* and *Center Stage*.

I hadn't seen either movie before or since that fifth-grade sleepover, but here's what my ten-year-old brain recorded to memory: girls with flat stomachs wearing halter tops, girls dancing on bars while men cheered, girls in leotards where you can see their nipples poking through and the girls not caring, something about cowboy hats and red mesh fabrics swirling around? To this day, the two movies are linked in my head as one big, horny film about thin, hot women gyrating to pop/rock/country music in bars and at ballet school. In my head, Julia Stiles stars in both movies. She is in neither.

I told my mom what we'd watched when I got home from the sleepover, probably recounting it in the same way I told her about Catherine P.'s sex-ed lesson. Though I'd learned what being horny was from watching it on-screen and, in turn, experiencing it personally, I still hadn't comprehended the idea of keeping secrets from my parents. I wasn't allowed to sleep over at Brittany S.'s again.

Sex is a thing parents do to have a baby and ew, oh my god, did my parents do that???

When I got my period at age eleven, my mom asked if I "knew what that meant." To which I was like, *Yes for sure duh I know everything I am ELEVEN after all.* I remember her asking me to explain to her what I thought sex was. I don't remember what I told her, but clearly she wasn't convinced as she responded by handing me a little pink booklet about menstruation and changing bodies. It was, as I'd suspected, the same booklet my mom received in the seventies when she first got her period.

There were vintage-looking illustrations of a white girl with pigtails staring at her undressed body in the mirror. I flipped to a section in the back that had a calendar titled something like "tracking your cycle," which is when I promptly closed the tiny book.

Who cares if "periods = sex." I have to bleed out my privates AND do homework about it?! No thanks. I'll pass.

The phrase "sexy sex-filled breasts" is a real thing that horny people say.

I spent the next couple of years feeling perpetual waves of horniness and having zero idea what to do about it. I wanted both everyone and no one to know what I knew about sex, which was still relatively little factual information. I had impulses to expend my sexual energy but didn't really know how other than screaming, "I HAVE SEXUAL ENERGY!!!"

Once, during this intermittent time, I was hanging outside my family's house with my siblings and our neighbor, a boy a year older than I was. I had an old dictionary with me in the front yard—very cool and casual, me!—and flipped to the "s" section of the book. I turned to find the page with the word "sex" because I hadn't ever heard of "subtlety" (that's a couple of pages later in the dictionary). Making sure I was in earshot of my older neighbor, I loudly sighed and said, "Ugh, it doesn't even have the *good* definition."

More than once, I stole socks and a bra from my mom's dresser to essentially play "boobs." I'd lock myself in the bathroom, put on my mom's bra (which was bigger and therefore hornier than mine), and stick balled up socks in each cup to fill it out. I did this over all my clothes and with zero awareness about the Oedipus-adjacent complex I was living out.

The orgasm-less climax of this confusing pent-up sexual energy happened while bopping around on the extremely old computer my dad had set up in the basement. It was an old, boxy Macintosh that barely had a functioning word processor. Our family only kept it to use as a play computer in the basement because my dad never throws away anything ever. Sometimes I would play around on the computer's calculator, adding 1 + 1 and hitting "equals" as fast as I could, seeing how high I could get the sum to go and how quickly. (The things I found boring and the things I found exciting in middle school are almost indistinguishable.) One time, while going to open the calculator application, I noticed another app I hadn't ever opened labeled "phone."

I knew this computer wasn't connected to the internet or a phone line and that the "phone" function had no way of actually working. So, I decided to play "phone." In the same way you can track someone's internet rabbit hole by going through their browser history, you could see my game of "phone" progress from dipping a toe (dialing our home number) to playfully splashing (dialing "911") to flirtatiously splashing ("calling" Taylor, a cute boy whose number I'd memorized with the intention to never call him ever—very normal and chill!) to swan diving into soaking wet oblivion. When I realized you could type letters into the phone, I lost my horny mind and "called" every boy I'd ever had a crush on. Then, pulse racing in my chest and my pants, I typed the words "sexy sex-filled breasts" and pressed "call."

Did I think "sex-filled breasts" were a real, physical thing? Did I hear the phrase "heaving bosom" once and decide to take some creative liberties? Did I want a pair of boobs to answer the phone???

To my simultaneous relief and dismay, nothing happened. As if "sexy sex-filled breasts" hadn't maxed out the horny words I knew, I went to type some more. When I did, a dropdown list of every number and phrase I'd typed popped up. I panicked.

I closed out the application and re-opened it. "Sexy sex-filled breasts" was still there. I restarted the computer and opened the phone app back up. Still saw "sexy sex-filled breasts"—again, the words, not a picture. I typed in a bunch of gibberish, "called" a bunch of fake numbers, hoping to push "breasts" off the list. They remained.

I resigned to the fact that I would inevitably be found out. That my parents, who would certainly have the impulse to use the nonfunctioning phone application on this barely function-ing computer, would see my "sexy sex-filled breasts" and dis-own me or banish me to hell or both. I wish I could go back and tell twelve-year-old me not to fear or feel ashamed, that literally no one would find out about my "sexy sex-filled breasts" until I wrote it down eight times in this book.

ATTENTION TARGET SHOPPERS: THIS STORE IS NOW RIFE WITH SEXUAL TENSION

While recently checking out at Target, the cashier struck up a conversation with me and asked what I was drinking. This is a pretty standard Target experience. Because it was near the holidays and because I am exactly the kind of person you think I am, I was drinking a peppermint mocha I bought at the Starbucks inside the store. She misheard me or misinterpreted me or mistook me for someone much bolder and, for some reason, thought I was referring to my vagina as a "peppermint mocha." I still am not sure what the fuck that even means. Our conversation ended with her telling me to make sure I get someone to "drink" my "peppermint mocha" because "it's Christmas" and I deserve it. It is the best sexual education I have ever received. Anyways, I have a theory that Target stores are corporately obligated to be extremely sexual. This is what a realistic store announcement would sound like. Please read it aloud in a breathy, perky, and kind of horny way.

* * *

Hey, Target Shoppers! Just a reminder that the store will be closing in twelve hours. You may think this is a premature announcement, but we know how much you like to take your time wink wink and also nudge nudge. We do understand how these Target runs often go: you come with the intention to quickly grab laundry detergent and toothpaste, get summoned by the siren call of our clearance racks, eventually finding your limbs entangled in a mess of 80-percent-off plaids and thin cardigans with small pockets. Suddenly, it's 10 p.m., you've abandoned your spouse and children, and still haven't made your way to the Tide Pods. We want to make sure you have plenty of time to stare longingly at a pair of $10.99 fake Keds, biting your lip while whispering, "I *shouldn't* . . . should I?"

We know you don't think of this as just another shopping trip; it's some much needed "me time." At Target, we know the only places women find a moment for themselves are in giant bubble baths or while retail shopping. Target is one of those places where a woman can really let her guard down. It is perhaps the only space she feels safe enough to spend a full twenty minutes lost in a manicured fantasy as she touches one of our seven thousand bottles of nail polish. Men shop with a purpose (tires, sports pants, beef jerky, condoms). Women shop for pleasure (shoes to look at but not walk in, blouses that caress you in places no man ever would, big zucchini but not for the reason you're thinking).

We've just been informed of a situation in aisle 7 where a group of Target shoppers (known as an "orgy") have fallen into an endless loop of complimenting each other's handbags back and forth. Please do not use this as an invitation to go to aisle 7 and look at the bags. Yes, they are from Target, and yes, they were on sale.

In the meantime, have you signed up for a Target RedCard yet? What about our Cartwheel coupons? Are you familiar with Target's rewards program? That's the one where we make sure our fitting room attendants don't judge you for trying on a mountain of $8.99 tees that will shrink the second you put them on at home. A new shirt feels as good as sex if you've never experienced sexual pleasure even once.

Looking for a gift for your friend's baby shower? A card for your friend's birthday? A quick romantic fling built around a shared love of discount jeggings? What about buy four, get one free super plus boxes of tampons, you capitalist li'l skank? Target has everything you need and even more things you don't but will buy anyway. Plus, screaming about how they got their pants on sale is as close as most straight women ever get to cumming.

Make sure you don't miss our Archer Farms brand pasta deal! For a limited time only (which starts right now and ends when the world does) you can get a $5 Target gift card when you buy just thirteen boxes of dry macaroni. You're not going to find a deal like that at Walmart! Lick our ass, Amazon! What are you going to do with that much macaroni? Who cares! It's about the experience you'll get *in* the store when the woman behind you in the checkout line demurely asks, "Did you get that on sale?" And you'll turn around, flirtatiously bat your eyelashes, and say, "I always do."

Here at Target, we do things a little differently. We know that straight men have space to express their sexuality through things like actual sex. Ladies, on the other hand, have chocolate commercials, Venus razors, the idea of a buff man standing near an ironing board, long-wear lipstick, eating a muffin with chocolate chips in it to "be a little bad," gently touching swaths of soft fabric, shiny hair that holds a curl, slimming tunics, and perfume samples.

Sorry, did you say you were looking for . . . *lube*. Shh, shh, keep your voice down. Yeah, of course we sell *lube*—we're Target. We've got everything. If you can't find something you're looking for in store (vibrators, erotic massagers, something that looks like lipstick but definitely isn't) or something you're too ashamed by your female sexuality to buy (see aforementioned list), Target .com has everything you need that you don't want to make eye contact with another person in order to get.

Thank you for shopping at Target. Expect More. Pay Less. Fingerbang a Glade candle at a discounted price.

HOW TO DATE ONLINE

I came of age in the early '00s when chat rooms were associated with the seedy underbelly of cyberspace and AOL mailed free internet minutes they stuck inside CD-ROMs somehow. Dating apps were barely a twinkle in a future Silicon Valley bro's eye when I was learning about the dos and don'ts of dating. If you would have told twelve-year-old Mia that now we all use full names and email addresses and put daily pictures of ourselves online, twelve-year-old Mia's parents would have overheard you and been like, "The internet cannot know your last name or see your face! Do you want to die?!?"

I was twenty-four and fresh out of a long-term relationship—one in which I'd felt lonely and stagnant and ready for newness—when I first saw dating apps as a viable option. A couple of my friends said I should try Tinder, giving me permission to do a thing I definitely wanted to do. I'd said I wanted something new and that's basically Tinder's business model: a brand-new person on your phone every time you swipe. Creating an account with a group of friends rather than alone in my living room took some of the sad and lonely "me want dick!!!" energy out of the process. Out of a combination of curiosity and the deep and constant desire for affirmation, I created a profile.

I had Tinder for an entire fifteen days. If I had to guess based on my experience and the comparative experience of friends and family, this is the perfect amount of time to be on Tinder. In that two-ish weeks, I learned a lot about the single, twenty-four- to thirty-year-old men in the greater Kansas City area. Too much, some might say. (Me. Me would say that.) For example:

1. You can just be a person in the world who lists "Travelling Cunnilingist" on a dating app profile. There is a person in the world—specifically within zero to twenty-five miles of my world—who had that as the entire contents of his bio.

1.1 To be fair, my entire bio was just a pizza emoji. (It's called being aloof and chill and in total denial about your lack of either. Ever heard of it?) Both the Travelling Cunnilingist and I exist on the same spectrum of terrible dating app profiles. I will say, though, that I rarely trust a straight man who is adamant about how much he *loves* to go down on women. Like it's some act of bravery or he's a feminist activist. Like his willingness to, God forbid, please a woman is symbol of his allyship. No thank you. I would rather fuck myself.

2. If you've never had the pleasure/curse of looking at a dating app, everything people say about straight men's pictures* is true. I can't tell you the number of

---

* Additionally, every city in the US falls somewhere on the "body of water/body of a fish" photo spectrum. Example: Kansas City has a high density of man-with-fish photos. Every man in Chicago is legally obligated to have a picture near Lake Michigan.

dogs and national monuments, guys with girls they claim they aren't dating, and guys with children they adamantly specify they haven't fathered I swiped through in a mere fifteen days.

3. My racial ambiguity is an icebreaker that transcends every space, as evidenced by one of the first messages I got, which read, "Three tries to guess each other's ethnicity?" I gave him exactly zero.

4. While I did not match with the guy whose hobbies and interests were exclusively "butt rubs and pizza," I now have the title for my new mixtape.

5. You think you've seen it all, and then you see someone who's used two of their five pictures to pay homage to their deceased mother with screenshotted Snapchat photos that read "RIP MOMMY" in red swoopy lettering. Also, now I've got to add "Future children must create mini-obituaries for me in any and all dating profiles" to my will.

6. A moment of clarity came when I was presented with a person who, at the end of a long "About Me" that listed his appreciation for standard interests like sports and travel and coffee, ended his bio with, "I prefer the original definition of marriage." Homophobia was as crucial and casual a part of his personality as having been to Cabo once. And while I had zero intention of swiping right, I STILL CLICKED THROUGH HIS PICTURES.

   His bio was like, "People of the Jury of Tinder Mia's Brain: We all know what kind of person I am, or at the very least, what kind of person I want to present myself as. We all know this will go nowhere given my loud stance against marriage equality. Or perhaps by "original definition of marriage" I mean the one in which a woman is viewed as the property of a man. Or maybe the one where you give a guy a goat and are then entitled to all his daughters or something like that. Whatever the case may be, all parties present know this would never and should never work out. Buuut, like, you should probably just check my pics to see if I have any where I'm not wearing a hat or you can see my face from a different angle."

After swiping right on a few profiles that weren't entirely horrifying, I went on a total of two dates. The first was very okay, which I've since learned is a success story in terms of Tinder dates. The second was equally okay until he pulled out his didgeridoo.

That's not a euphemism. My date took out a literal didgeridoo and just . . . started playing it. I'd turned around for a second to pet his dog (also not a euphemism), and when I looked back, there he was, nose-deep in a didgeridoo. If you're not familiar, didgeridoos are long, tubular instruments. There's some debate about whether they're in the wind or brass family. There is zero debate about whether they're something you just whip out thirty minutes after you meet someone.

Not to sound inexperienced, but this was the first time I'd heard a didgeridoo in person. The noise was startling, to say the least. I'm not sure what warning he could have given other than "Wanna hear what it'd sound like if a boat had a sinus infection?" If you've ever been surprised by a baritone fart that somehow sounded kind of nasally, you know exactly what it's like to suddenly hear a didgeridoo.

If you're wondering where you even look when someone is playing an intimate didgeridoo concert, the answer is I still don't know. Eye contact seemed intrusive, but staring right at the didgeridoo seemed worse? I'm familiar with the awkward romantic serenade—no straight woman attends a liberal arts college without hearing "Can I play 'Wonderwall' for you?" from an English major named Brenden at least once—but the didgeridoo is not particularly melodic. It's more like "Can I play this one sustained note from 'Wonderwall' for you?"

Still, my date continued to proudly bellow on the instrument—a four-foot-long instrument that he brought home on a plane from Australia—that he'd later tell me he's "dabbling in."

"Oh . . . okay," I said after my date finished his song/note.

"Do you want to play it?" he asked, sincerely, with no hint of innuendo whatsoever.

We didn't go on a second date, and I deleted Tinder pretty soon after. This is, in great part, because I met Riley a few days after the didgeridoo date. Had I not met Riley, I'd probably still be on Tinder, eventually having swiped right on the Travelling Cunnilingist and using my proficiency with the didgeridoo to cover my deep sobs of loneliness.

It's strange how lonely casual dating can be. But being lonely in a relationship is equally strange. It's very "alone in a crowded room," but that crowded room is just two people on a couch watching Netflix on separate devices and asking what the other wants to do for dinner back and forth forever. However, that loneliness also comes with the comfort of knowing you're with someone who at least cares about you to some degree. There is zero comfort or care in Tinder or its dating app ilk.

Sitting alone in your dark bedroom, a glass of wine in hand, expressionlessly swiping through profiles is one of the most isolating ways to meet people. However, playing Tinder—let's not kid ourselves, Tinder is basically Candy Crush, but the candy is dicks—with friends in the room with me was more fun than I should admit. It was like the board game Dream Phone but Steve isn't just on a playing card; he's real and has a shirtless picture and oh my god, he's messaging you right now.

The second I opened up Tinder when I was by myself, I felt a familiar kind of loneliness. It was one I'd felt years before when I spent nights sitting on Omegle for hours. If you weren't in college in the early 2010s, you likely missed the random video chat website phenomenon. Sites like Chatroulette and Omegle would access your microphone, webcam, and last shred of innocence and randomly pair two users up to video chat. What could possibly go wrong with that?

My friend Sami, who taught me what sperm isn't and has seen me cry onstage to "Wind Beneath My Wings," introduced me to Omegle a few weeks before I left for a summer-long internship in San Francisco. Playing Omegle with Sami was extremely fun. Our Omegle game went like this: We'd try to find someone to talk to, telling each other we'd be down to chat with "literally anyone who seems cool!" while both separately hoping to find random groups of college boys to flirt at. We'd begin clicking, hoping we wouldn't be randomly paired up with someone showing their penis (oh wow shock gasp can you believe that's what these sites eventually turned into?), and screaming whenever we inevitably saw a stranger's penis.

Omegle was my pre-Tinder Tinder. During that summer in San Francisco, I would spend a humiliating amount of time clicking "new" to generate a random video chat. Then, I'd start a riveting dialogue with strangers like "Hey" and "What's up?" The only time I have ever experienced an earthquake, I was video chatting with someone on Omegle. I thought a car had hit my aunt and uncle's house and I ran out of the room to see what happened. When I returned, house and humans unharmed, the guy I was chatting with didn't believe I'd just experienced a minor earthquake. He thought I was trying to find a reason to hang up, called me a bitch, and hung up on me.

Unless you gave any identifying information to whoever you were chatting with, ending the video chat had no consequences. You were anonymous, aside from the part where you showed your full face and whatever bits of your body you felt like. It was the perfect place for me to get instant affirmation from people far too old or far too young to be affirming me.

A real low came when I spent a good half hour getting ready to go on Omegle. The best part about being a woman is not our prerogative to have a little fun, but how ingrained the concept of "natural beauty" is in our brains. I know how much makeup to put on so I don't look like I'm wearing makeup but I still register as "woman." I know how to do my hair so I can say, "Oh, it just does this on its own" and have most straight men go, "Cool." I signed onto Omegle that night looking my natural best.

I began the night by closing one chat in a panic, thinking I'd somehow matched someone I went to high school with. This was an international website. The likelihood of that actually happening is laughable but did not assuage my "Oh no I've been found out" fears. After clicking past more anonymous penises than anyone should ever see, I eventually started chatting with a guy who I thought was cute. My type, for the record, is any man who will look at me. We realized we were the same age, had similar interests, were both doing internships away from home, and were very, very lonely. The last was an unspoken commonality.

We typed back and forth for a few hours on Omegle, our cameras enabled but microphones turned off. I could justify revealing my entire face, a small portion of my bedroom, and the intentional hint of a bra strap to this stranger. But letting him hear my voice? Nope, too personal. In the chat space, we asked each other a range of extremely innocuous to humiliatingly personal questions with zero transitions. It was the kind of conversation you only feel comfortable having with a stranger when you're nineteen and desperately alone. Eventually, we exchanged Skype names and started video chatting there. After Skyping for a couple weeks, we exchanged phone numbers. We spent the next couple months texting each other all day and video chatting for hours nearly every night.

There isn't a convincing way to say "All we did was talk" without it sounding like a lie, but truly, all we did was talk. It was exactly what my nineteen-year-old self craved: a boy (!) who would talk (!!) to ME (!!!). It was the kind of connection every person has at least once early into college, where you both are like, "You're so much different than everyone else. They're all fake and you're real." It felt like the first time maybe ever that I liked someone and they liked me back equally.

The fact that at the end of the summer I flew across the country to meet a stranger I met through Omegle is both wildly uncharacteristic and extremely me. My parents were as concerned as you would expect parents to be when their nineteen-year-old daughter says, "I'm flying to Texas to meet a boy I met on the internet. He's real, I promise!" He was real, and he was late picking me up from the airport.

We spent five days together in his hometown, just the two of us. I remember it feeling magical and exciting and quietly adding "Texas" to the mental list of places I might live after college. I remember walking through a botanical garden, giggling through an art museum, and driving through a Sonic drive-through, all three feeling equally romantic. I remember telling my mom and my sister how great he was, how much I liked him, how it seemed like he actually liked me, too.

I remember, when I recounted my trip to friends, brushing over the amount of time he and I spent brainstorming fake backstories for me, God forbid someone he knew saw us out together. "I'll say I'm from . . . Philadelphia?" I suggested thinking it sounded cool but vague. I tried to remember, sitting on the plane ride home, what his face looked like when he asked me to stay in his room after neighbors unexpectedly showed up at his house. "It was probably so I didn't feel awkward," I remember convincing myself, like pretending to not exist behind a bedroom door was a normal occurrence. And though I committed to memory the night the girl he'd told me was his ex showed up at his house unexpectedly and he asked me to play invisible in his bedroom again, I didn't tell anyone about it.

Our pseudo-relationship fizzled almost as soon as it began. About a month after our first meeting, we met for the second and last time. I flew to his college town one weekend after school started, excited to meet his friends and pretend the two of us met "through a random mutual." As we stayed cooped up in his fraternity house bedroom, running out of things to talk about, I realized something was off. He didn't want the two of us to hang out with any of his friends, which was difficult because he lived in a frat house. He didn't want classmates seeing us out eating together, a nearly impossible feat in a college town. After the second night of sitting on his twin bed, I realized he didn't want people to meet me, the physical embodiment of how lonely he had been this summer. I both resented the instinct and understood it entirely.

When I flew back to Wisconsin, our long-distance chatting turned from something I looked forward to into a chore I felt like I was convincing him to do. I learned that he and his ex maybe hadn't fully broken up. I realized he was never going to call me his girlfriend. I knew the relationship was officially over when I drunkenly texted him "happy new year" and he responded with something like, "k."

I haven't casually dated enough to have any real advice for anyone stuck in the lonely rut that often is casual dating. In case you need a recap, I only spent two weeks on Tinder, and I also bought a $300 plane ticket to meet up with someone from Omegle. My dating experience exists on the two extremes of the casual dating spectrum. Sometimes dating feels like hopping between different kinds of loneliness. Sometimes you spend half a year video chatting with a stranger and realize you've learned a lot about yourself in the process. I learned that I am more spontaneous than I believed myself to be. Also, I'm a natural at the didgeridoo.

TREATING OBJECTS LIKE WOMEN

Hey, Remote. What are you doing way over there? Why don't you come over here so I can treat you like a remote deserves to be treated? What I mean is, I'm going to push your buttons. But, like, really well. I said I'm gonna push your buttons really well! Why are you ignoring me, Remote? Are you calling me lazy? Think I can't get up and turn you on? I mean, turn the TV on. See, now you got me all flustered. It wasn't a compliment or anything because I'm pretty sure TVs require you to use the remote in order to even change the channel now. So, shut up, whatever. I WANTED TO WATCH NETFLIX ON MY COMPUTER ANYWAY.

Damn, Bathroom Floor. Are you trying to kill me looking like that? Because a lot of accidental deaths occur in the bathroom. I bet I could make you so wet after I took a shower and realized I should really buy a bath mat and shower curtains and maybe a more absorbent towel.

What's up, Netflix? Where's that square-faced smile I like? You down to marathon? What do you mean, "Am I still watching?" Yeah, I'm still watching. You can't tell me not to watch. It's a free country. I can still watch. Don't put the entirety of the *Final*

Destination franchise in my face if you don't want me to watch all five movies at once. Again, it is a free country, and you can't take that right away. Who do you think you are? Hulu? YOU'RE NO HULU.

Hulu. Hey, Hulu. Whoa, whoa hold on—why'd you just throw out that you're "subscription-only" now? Maybe I have a subscription somewhere else. Maybe I wasn't even looking to watch anything. Maybe I was just checking to see if you have any updates to your user interface. I can do that without a subscription. Not everybody that checks your site is looking for a subscription. I didn't even bring up subscriptions. You did. And you know that I could get your log-in information if I wanted to. I could get the log-in information of literally any subscription-based streaming service here, SO YOU SHOULD BE HAPPY I EVEN CAME TO YOU, DAMN.

I wish you had a twin, Sock I Found Under the Couch.

Hey, Cutie. Oh, you're one of those Halo oranges? My bad.

You come to this little spot often, Roomba?

Smile more, Mirror.

I'm gonna tear you up for real, Expired Coupon from Target for a Toothpaste I Never Buy.

Excuse me, Leftovers in the Back of the Fridge? I was just wondering what you are. Like, where are you from? Are you Chinese? No? Are you sure? Are you Mexican? You look like you could be Mexican. You sure you're not Mexican? I have a lot of friends who go to Mexican restaurants, so I can usually tell. Oh, are you from one of those Asian fusion restaurants? I just want to know because I love Asian fusion restaurants. I DON'T CARE THAT I CAN'T HAVE YOU BECAUSE YOU'RE MY ROOMMATE'S LEFTOVERS. JUST TELL ME WHAT YOU ARE, BITCH.

A NICE PIECE OF SATIRE
YOU CAN TAKE
HOME TO YOUR PARENTS

You make a trip home to visit your parents, and they ask the question you've been dreading: "So . . . have you been seeing any new satirical articles lately?"

Of course you have. You're reading the best satire of your life. With modern technology and social networking, you have access to more humor than your parents could have imagined when they were your age. You're a young adult, living in a blue city, with a presence on every major social media platform. All you do is skim satirical articles.

But you can't tell them that. Your parents don't want to hear about the night you spent cozied up to a Twitter thread accurately comparing Trump to a misbehaving toddler (and not just because you can't even remember the handle of the person who tweeted it). You and your parents want very different things in a piece of humor. And it's nearly impossible to find a McSweeney's in the sheets and a syndicated *Modern Family* episode in the streets.

Remember Chewbacca Mom? God, they loved Chewbacca Mom. Why can't you find something that's like Chewbacca Mom but just words? Maybe you could watch Chewbacca Mom on mute and read the captions together? That has to be some form of social commentary you can agree on, right?

Nobody wants a repeat of the time your parents caught you swiping through headlines on The Onion, and you made the mistake of thinking it'd be something you could enjoy together. You had to keep explaining this isn't what people are talking about when they call something "fake news." Then it became this whole thing when they realized you don't actually read the articles. ("How can you even know anything about a piece when you're swiping so quickly?!")

As open-minded as your parents want to say they are, they're just not going to like an imagined dialogue between Melania Trump and the Statue of Liberty, two women designed as decorative gifts from foreign nations. They want someone dressed as the Statue of Liberty reading the Declaration of Independence in Melania's voice. To which you'll say you want something with a sense of humor. And they'll say that does have a sense of humor. And now you're watching Chewbacca Mom for the fiftieth time.

This is usually when your mom brings up something she saw on Facebook. "Did you see your cousin Bethany found the perfect mash-up of a golden retriever dancing to that song from *Trolls*? Doesn't she just seem so happy?" You ask if she means Bethany or the golden retriever. Nobody laughs.

You'll have to remind yourself their intentions are good when they try setting you up with Aunt Jacqueline's email chain. You didn't even know you had an Aunt Jacqueline, let alone want to commit to her weekly messages probably filled with screenshots of the Yahoo! home page. Regardless, you say you'll think about it.

You know they just want you to be happy, even if they'll never see what you see in someone like John Oliver. Perhaps one day, you'll run into an essay when you least expect it, and it'll make you laugh in a way you haven't in a while. A piece that somehow agrees with you politically without seeming political at all. A piece that transcends bubbles while still acknowledging them. And you'll think, "I can't wait to tell my parents about you." Until then, you'll always have Chewbacca Mom.

I DON'T KNOW
HOW TO BE A BRIDE

Riley and I got engaged in the summer of 2017. We were both in bed—him about to go to sleep, me doing a crossword puzzle—when he started playing what I thought was a podcast. This is pretty standard for our nightly routine. Yes, it is very cute, and yes, you should clap. The podcast sounded weird and I didn't recognize it, so I asked Riley, "What is this?" Then the theme song to Phoebe Robinson and Jessica Williams's *2 Dope Queens* started playing, and I said, "Oh, okay," and went back to my crossword.

Then the episode started talking about Tinder and didgeridoos, something extremely specific to my experience with Tinder. The "podcast" was actually a mash-up of sorts that Riley made, combining clips from our favorite songs and shows and Michelle Obama speeches into one aural love fest. If you're wondering what the whitest way to get engaged is, it's through a custom podcast. I can say that because I am half-white and have lots of friends who do podcasts. His proposal was essentially a twenty-five-minute audio tour of all our inside jokes. It ended with a bunch of voicemail messages from family and friends from all parts of my life. It is still the best gift I've ever received, and it still makes me sob. If you listened to it you'd probably be like, "I don't get it."

He proposed using this shitty ring I found in our silverware drawer that I'd wear sometimes because my taste, like the ring, is shitty. We planned on exchanging actual rings at the wedding ceremony after a conversation about getting married months before the proposal.* The conversation went something like this:

HIM: Do you want an engagement ring?

ME: Do you have to wear an engagement ring *and* a wedding ring?

HIM: I don't know.

ME: That seems like too many rings.

HIM: Okay.

We thought about both of us exchanging faux engagement rings, but we quickly realized that would require just so much explanation to all our family. I'm sure there is some traditional, beautiful, patriarchal reason why women get engagement rings and men don't, but I don't want my Google ads to be heteronormative nonsense and T-shirts that say "HE LIKED IT SO HE PUT A RING ON IT" for the rest of forever. I already had to ex-

---

* The idea of being "surprised" by a proposal or "having no idea" an engagement is coming feeds into my exact brand of anxiety.

plain, every time someone asked to see the ring, why I didn't have an engagement ring, and no, I wasn't upset, and yes, I was sure.

The thing no one tells you about getting engaged is how quickly everyone asks you every single detail about the wedding. The questions are well-intentioned and kind, but also just so, so funny. Like, do you think in the twelve hours since we've been officially engaged we've nailed down a date, a venue, a caterer, who's invited, what we're wearing, and the seating arrangement? Could you imagine how truly bonkers that would be? People would call the cops.

While both Riley and I are very much planners, him admittedly more so than me, we knew little about planning an actual wedding. Especially in terms of what people expect out of a wedding.

To understand how little I know about wedding planning, once I brought taco dip to a wedding shower after misreading the invitation to an almost impressive degree. It said to bring your favorite vegetarian recipe. I, for some reason, misinterpreted that as "bring a dish to share." I showed up with a bag of Tostitos, a giant pan of taco dip, and zero actual gifts.

If you thought since that mishap I'd learned my wedding shower lesson, I assure you, I did not! More recently, I was at a bridal shower, surrounded by panties, prayer cards, and also the bride's grandmother, and all I wanted to do was scream, "WHAT IS EVEN GOING ON HERE?" I didn't, which, honestly, does show growth. However, the invitation said to bring a pair of cute panties in lieu of a card. My brain went "Cool, cool, so just the underwear then," and once again, I! Didn't! Bring! A GIFT!!!

This was far from a political act or something rooted in some personal vendetta; I honestly just didn't know how many and what type of gifts are expected in all the events leading up to a wedding. Also, what would you even do with seven silky bathrobes?!? If it's any consolation to the brides, these shining examples of me not understanding how to appropriately act at wedding showers is what keeps me up at night.

Riley and I had a co-ed wedding shower because a family friend was kind enough to organize one. We told people not to bring gifts because we already somehow had three toasters and did not need any more. Unlike me, everyone followed directions.

If you're in need of a good gift for any occasion—bridal shower, wedding, birthday, an apology for bringing taco dip when you weren't supposed to—I have one that is perfect for any and all celebrations: money. Just give the couple some money! I don't know who in the Bible Belt said money was a thoughtless gift, but I would like to talk to them, hand them a twenty, then take it away and ask who's thoughtless now. Having a Kitchen-Aid Stand Mixer does give me little homemaking butterflies in my stomach, but you know how else I can get a KitchenAid Stand Mixer? With some money that you give me!

Our wedding registry consisted of one item, and that item was money. Actually, it said to not worry about gifts since more than half our guests would be traveling for the wedding. However, if they *wanted* to give us something, our favorite color is cash.

The wedding planning process is so strange. You have to know how many people you want to invite before you can find a venue before you can figure out what food you're going to order before you can decide how much alcohol to buy. It's a party planning logic puzzle where the clues are like "Two of your aunts don't get along but you can't ask which ones" and "Your cousin said 'No bread' but you don't know if that's an allergy or a preference."

Riley and I planned our wedding together, pretty much just the two of us. This, I learned, was an anomaly. "That's so nice he's helping you plan!" people would say. "Wow, you're letting him make decisions?" they'd joke. Not because I'm some controlling, Type A, "I'm in charge of the group project" bitch. I mean, I am, but the assumption was that I, the female bride in this heterosexual union, would be doing the decision making for the wedding. I barely like deciding what to eat for dinner. The idea of being solely responsible for researching, narrowing down, and decided dozens of things for 120-plus people is my personal version of hell.

Luckily, we found this little-known wedding planning helper. It's called Google—ever heard of it? There are many things I don't understand how people did pre-internet: travel across the country, travel to other countries, plan a vacation, pay their taxes, figure out what they're going to eat for dinner or how to renew their driver's license or what Macaulay Culkin looks like today. Wedding planning sans internet would have either been an expensive nightmare or a weird house party in a church basement.

We also asked married friends and family their advice in the process of planning a wedding. We got a lot of "The *marriage* is what's the most important, not the wedding." That is nice and sweet and thoughtful but provided no real guidance as to how the fuck to decide which venue was right or which DJ seemed like they wouldn't play "Cupid Shuffle" on repeat.

Here is the one piece of advice I wish I'd been given: make a list of the things that are important to the two of you. Make another list of the things that are actually important to the people you love who are attending the wedding. I knew my dad would be bummed if we didn't do some sort of father-daughter dance, despite how weird and yucky and borderline "take these goats for my daughter" they can seem. However, I knew no one in my family would be like, "Hmm, I noticed you didn't do a garter toss, and your Uncle Steve was really looking forward to catching the lingerie you'd be wearing around your thigh all night."

Aside from that, do whatever the fuck you want. Want your wedding party to be immediate family only as to avoid weird conversations with distant friends? Go for it. You want to ban anyone from playing the "Chicken Dance" or any R. Kelly? You are free to do that as well. Want to make everyone stand and applaud when you enter the reception? They're going to do that anyway, so get ready.

We wanted our wedding to be fun. So we did the things we knew would make us happy, make our guests comfortable, and not make us completely broke or lose our minds. I think we did all three successfully. (There was the part during the reception where my sister and I drunkenly revived a dance we choreographed. So maybe we didn't fully do the second thing.)

At the time I'm writing this, Riley and I are coming up on our one-year anniversary. I'm not sure if the first anniversary is "paper" or "cotton" or "taco dip" or "panties." I know eating the top tier of your wedding cake you saved in the freezer is a thing, but we will not be doing that. Partly because that sounds freezer burn-y. But mostly because we got big-ass sheet cakes from

Costco that I drunkenly finished off the second we got home the night of our wedding.

I'm still getting used to saying I'm someone's wife. Turns out, I don't really know how to do that either. If you're looking for marriage or relationship advice, I have neither. A lot of people have a lot of thoughts, feelings, advice books, and religious cults on how to have a good marriage. To likely no one's surprise, ours has involved a lot of talking, listening, laughing, crying, patience, grace with each other, grace with ourselves, and pooping with the door open. Your mileage may vary.

Whatever you choose to do wedding-wise, I hope you end your big day feeling loved and in love, full of food and beverages and gratitude. I ended mine completely naked in my bathroom, barfing up cake and wine. It was perfect.

THE HOLY SACRAMENT
OF BIRTH CONTROL

Let us begin by making the sign of the cross, as praying you don't get pregnant is one of the few forms of birth control readily accessible to everyone. Receiving the sacrament of birth control is an exciting time in a person's life. You should feel proud, honored even. You're about to join a select part of the population anointed with hormone-suppressing oils, baptized in period-altering waters.

I see you've chosen the path of the intrauterine device, Mother IUD. I also see you've previously prayed to the Patron Saints of the Pill: Loestrin, Yaz, Mircette, and Yasmin. Like the troop of high school mean girls their names make them out to be, they may have led you into temptation: making your tits look amazing, giving you skin that had never been clearer, lightening the flow of your period a noticeable amount. You took them like your daily bread.

Then, came the plagues of Depression and Anxiety and Really Weird Poops. So goes the verse: *Love is patient, love is kind. Love is taking the pill every day even though it fucked you right up. For you so loved your only uterus and the freedom of family planning that you gave yourself weight gain, mood swings, nausea, inconsistent periods, and an underlying sense of dread.*

I want you to know that you are not alone. At least in the metaphorical sense. Unfortunately, the men you lie with will not be expected to put their bodies through such torture.

When you visit your gynecologist to receive your IUD, you will begin with the traditional greeting: "Forgive me, Doctor, for I have sinned. It has been three Tinder dates since my last visit." You will note that your last confession involved divulging that you had "an itchy vag," the biblical curse for sleeping with the second hottest guy in a local improv troupe. The best-case scenario, you confessed, was the itching was caused by a PH imbalance in your vagina, brought on by the Plan B you recently took.

Your unholy union with improv fuckboy involved the standard hymnal (him playing guitar at you for an uninterrupted forty-five minutes). He doused you with the liturgical sprinkling of his back sweat. You directed him to "please open your bedside table to page Condom" as today's service did not include you being on birth control. He was guided by some higher force to respond, "I'll pull out," which didn't match the words in your missalette.

Though you walked through the valley of his shadowy shared apartment, you feared no STIs: for you made his ass send you pictures of his latest screening. You prayed his timing while pulling out was better than when he played that Sufjan song.

When the ceremony ended, you dressed, genuflecting to collect your underwear from the floor. You made the pilgrimage to the sexual health section of CVS, like so many before you have. After a brief, private counsel with Youth Minister Google, you decided it was best to buy the name-brand version though it would be more expensive.

By the grace of Plan B, during your last confession, your gynecologist reassured you your test results were pure, absolving you of any lasting sin.

In preparation for the sacrament of the IUD, you will be expected to don the ceremonial garb: a medical gown and that weird, tiny half-sheet you never remember how to properly put on. You will pray you figure out how to wear the robe so both your boobs and your entire butt are covered but accessible if necessary, how to display the little blanket so your crotch is hidden but not wrapped up like a human burrito.

While you wait for your room's parishioners to return (the doctor, the nurse, in some cases an exorcist), you will find it is a good time to reflect. To take in the blessing of not worrying about getting pregnant. To mourn the passing of that terrible and specific smell of sex and latex, the one that christened your ex-boyfriend's roommate's futon so many years ago. To give thanks for that time in Target when you unexpectedly ran into a co-worker and she didn't notice the box of pregnancy tests in your basket. The latter, nothing short of a miracle.

Do not let your faith falter, even when you hear the nurse practitioner in the hallway chanting, "Hey Abby, is the nonhormonal IUD the copper one or the other one?" You will not ask why your room has an Anne Geddes Baby Ladybug doll sitting on the windowsill, like some sort of watchful mutant Christ-child. You will grant forgiveness to the pamphlets for other birth control methods which use cutesy marketing copy like "BREAK UP with your birth control. DEFINE THE RELATIONSHIP with your ovaries." You will prepare your body to receive the sacrament, putting your legs in the stirrups and your vagina in full view.

Then they will bring forth the gifts: a speculum, the ceremonial gel, and, finally, the IUD. Your doctor will ask the question for which you have been preparing, "Who gives this woman in marriage to this IUD?" To which you will respond, "I do."

"This is the thing that goes in your body," she will say, holding the IUD up eucharistically. Though it is a scary-looking, T-shaped contraption, you will respond, "Amen."

"This thing may affect your blood," she will continue, saying things like "heavier flow" and "worse cramps." You will swallow your fear and say, "Amen."

Your knees will part and the angel of a doctor will say, "You may feel a little pinch." Your body may writhe, your insides constricting, as though the devil is moving through you. In time, it will subside, I promise. And then, it will be over.

When you leave the room, you may feel terrible or not any different at all. You may wonder why people make such a big deal about this thing. I mean, "hallowed" and "hollowed" sound so similar. But this is an initiation into a new chapter in your life, a sacrament of self-love.

You may consummate the marriage by reaching inside yourself to see if you can feel the strings. You may fear you are alone, noticing that in your most troublesome times, there is only one set of footsteps in the sand. Yes, those are your own footsteps because you did not need to carry a child you were not ready for. You walk alone, and you are at peace.

As you continue on your journey, may you be blessed with heating pads and comfy blankets when the period cramps shake you to your core. Remember, you can do all things through alcohol, which numbs the emotional pain but supposedly makes those cramps worse. Let us end by praying, O Birth Control Gods, that the men we lie with don't sneakily take off their condoms, a thing that apparently some think is an okay thing to do. That is sacrilegious and extremely fucked up.

In the name of the pill, the patch, and the IUD, Amen.

Part 5

ON BEING

Human

These are stories about our inward-facing selves. Who we are at our core, what we feel, what we think. They are about the things that make us cry and laugh and scream. They're about why we think the way we do even when we want to be like, "Nah, I don't think like that." They're about the weird things we have to do to prove we're human to ourselves, to each other, to robots online. They're about the gross and real, strange yet standard, weird but ultimately normal parts of being a whole entire person.

LEARNING HOW
TO NOT SHIT MYSELF

Everybody has a shit story. That is true and a fact or at least a hill I am fully committed to dying on. I've bought property on this hill. I spend my weekends there, waving my flag and proudly belting the song of my people. Except the hill is just a big ol' turd mound, the flag is a pair of my own shit-stained underwear, and the song is a series of symphonic fart noises I make with my mouth like *braaaawmp thlrrrrpt*. Oh, I'm sorry—was that a wince of disgust I detected? Did that description become a little too visually arresting? Do you find poop talk gross and immature and not what you paid money to read? Well, Hon, maybe you need to grow up a little.

We're all adults here. And as adults, I think we can all admit to having one good story about pooping our pants when we were definitely too old to be doing so. Or at least a time in which we had an alarming close call. If you do not have a personal, pants-shitting tale in your storytelling arsenal, I regret to inform you that you are not yet an adult. I don't care what you know about mortgages and good Crock-Pot recipes or how many children and

Roth IRAs you have. You become an adult when you poop your pants, and those are the rules.

I have shit myself once. The experience, in three words/short phrases: Lowe's, paint aisle, uneventful. It happened more recently than I should probably admit in print, but oh well, here we are. My butt was ready for something the rest of my body wasn't, and that's really the end of that. If you're going to sit there and tell me that worse things *haven't* happened in the paint aisle of a Lowe's home improvement and hardware store, sorry but you're wrong. That, however, is not The Shit Story™. That experience occurred in the summer of 1999.

I was eight, which is young in terms of coming-of-age moments, but wise beyond my years in terms of not pooping my pants. My dad and I were on a final tour of the home our family would soon be moving into. It's a ranch-style home in suburban Wisconsin where I spent the majority of my childhood and where my parents still live. The exterior is this orange-yellow-red brick that kind of looks like when you mix ketchup, mayo, and mustard together—the official color of the Midwest. The interior has all the parts you'd expect a home to have: a kitchen part, a living room part, a few bedrooms, and a couple bathrooms. It's unassuming and cozy and, now, a little bit cramped when all six members of my family are back in it together.

About halfway through the tour—of this single-story, ranch-style home—I felt a feeling. It was a stomach feeling and not a happy stomach feeling like love butterflies or that feeling you get when you're about to eat really good pad thai. (Not that those two feelings are mutually exclusive. I've been spiritually moved by pad thai before.)

I felt that universal stomach feeling known to humankind as: I am about to shit my pants.

Again, this was not a large house and this was not our first or second or probably even third time going through it. We'd seen it in all its suburban, ranch-style glory, and my dad had just come to finalize a few details. This tour could not have been more than fifteen minutes long—twenty if we're being generous with how long my dad may have talked about crown molding. But in the moment, my body had no concept of time.

I've never been an outspoken person, but I was especially quiet when I was a kid. In fifth grade, I started a presentation on space exploration by standing at the front of the classroom, staring at my trifold board completely silent for a solid minute until my teacher was like, "Well, are you gonna tell us about the astronaut chimps or what?" So I'm sure I didn't openly announce to my dad and the previous homeowner, who was giving the tour, that I needed to use the bathroom ASAP. I'm guessing that I, instead, spent a minute or five too long continuing to saunter around the house, nodding quietly like, "Ah, yes, I *can* tell this is new carpet, Harold. That is the only thing I am thinking about right now and absolutely nothing else. Like, for example, how the entire insides of my body might come out of my butt at any moment. I mean—oh, wow, Harold, this carpet."

Thankfully, I eventually must have mustered up enough courage to excuse myself from our three-person tour group. I left to unleash my demons in the privacy of what was still technically some stranger's bathroom. My friends, sex is great but have you ever thought you were about to poop your pants and then made it to the toilet on time? The relief—emotionally, psychologically, physically—is poetic.

However, what happened next must have been poetic justice for some shit-related crime I had committed in another life: there was no toilet paper.

I panic-waddled around the bathroom, looking like a shameful penguin with my pants at my ankles. I quietly but quickly opened cabinets and drawers, hoping to find a spare roll, some tissue, maybe a towel no one would miss. But my search left me with only dental floss and a plastic baggie.

The floss seemed far too tedious, and wiping my ass with a Ziploc bag sounded like a humiliating thing to have to explain to a doctor after inevitably slicing my asshole on one of the sharp top corners.

So, I did what anyone would do in that situation: I wiped my butt with my underwear.

If you've never found yourself in a situation where you've needed to fashion toilet paper out of miscellaneous bathroom objects, like some kind of disgusting MacGyver, let me tell you: it is amazing what the human spirit is capable of in times of distress. I used my underwear like flower-patterned cloth toilet paper, which is extremely foul . . . but also kind of fancy? When have you ever wiped your butt with a floral-patterned cotton cloth? How posh! How chic! Do you think that's what the Queen uses to wipe?

I finished doing that nasty, bad, bad deed as best I was able, threw my underwear away, and kept living my life as normally as I could.

Ha ha, just kidding! I didn't do that because hell hath no end and there was no trash can in the bathroom. It was just me, my underwear, and whatever remained of my eight-year-old dignity.

(Side note: Why did the previous homeowner's top packing priorities include toilet paper and a garbage can? Aren't those the literal last things you'd want to remove from your home??? The items missing from the bathroom felt prescient in way that attacked me personally.) Fortunately, I did have enough of a grasp of the situation to know that flushing my underwear down the toilet would be more of a problem than a solution. However, that still left me with evidence to dispose of and no proper trash receptacle in sight.

So I did what anyone would do in that situation: Put my makeshift underwear toilet paper into the aforementioned Ziploc baggie, shoved the baggie into my pants, smoothed out my pants, and pulled my shirt over the lumpy area as to not give away what terrible secrets lay beneath. Then I left the bathroom, hoping no one would stand too closely or breathe too deeply near me. That dental floss is probably still in the back of the bathroom cabinet, forever changed by the afternoon, as was I.

I probably should have won an award for Being the Most Chill and Nonchalant While Taking a House Tour with Shit-Stained Underwear Shoved Inside a Baggie Inside My Pants. Not to be an advertisement for Ziploc, but that double-lock seal is no joke: nobody smelled a thing. At least, nobody gave any indication that they smelled a thing. Maybe that previous homeowner is somewhere writing a story called, "Learning How to Ignore an Eight-Year-Old Who Definitely Shit Herself."

The three of us continued our tour outside, my plastic sandwich-turned-underwear-trash bag still in tow. As my dad and the homeowner were deep in conversation about who knows what—I, as you might imagine, was a little too preoccupied to keep track of anything other than my underwear—I saw a beacon of hope in the form of a woodpile. And yes, my friends, I did what anyone would do in that situation: I secretly hid the baggie with the poop panties underneath the pile of firewood.

Our tour ended, my dad and I left, and I shoved that memory deep within my eight-year-old brain, planning never to speak of the horrific things I'd done to that Ziploc baggie or that woodpile ever again.

That is until about 2005. I was a sophomore in high school and contained six more years' worth of humiliating memories (including all of middle school) buried deep within my easily embarrassed psyche. I'd never spoken of The Incident to anyone—my family, a friend, the pages of a diary, or a compassionate vagabond—forcing myself to forget about it completely.

So, of course, when my dad called us all out to the backyard, where he'd just finished disassembling the woodpile that had been in place since we first moved in, I was initially just as confused by the object he beheld: a small Ziploc bag stuffed with a pair of girls' underwear, patterned with small blue flowers and smears of, what appeared to be, shit.

In hindsight, it looked like a crime scene. This is perhaps the only situation in which saying "Oh, that's just my poopy underwear from 1999" would bring sighs relief. The events eventually all came rushing back to me in the way that my diarrhea probably rushed to my lower intestines on that fateful day: slowly, then all at once.

I'd been found out, betrayed by the actions of my former self. Had I acted sloppily? I mean, yeah, duh, I did an *extremely* sloppy thing. All things considered, this is exactly how it had to end. *Of course* I'd gotten sudden-onset sour butt (the scientific term) during the only twenty minutes of that day I wasn't at home. *Of course* there hadn't been any toilet paper. *Of course* there was no garbage can. *Of course* I had to shamefully shove my soiled underwear into my pants and then dispose of them under a woodpile. And *of course* my dad—the only member of my family who was with me on the day of The Incident—had to find my hidden poo-poo secret. There was no other way this could have ended.

My family is comfortable talking about bodily functions like a dog is comfortable licking itself whenever and in front of whomever. It's second nature. It's at the core of who we are and how we connect with each other, and if you happen to be in the room when my brother farts, Guy I Just Started Dating, welcome to the family, I guess. Please laugh accordingly.

My family found what had been one of the most traumatizing poop-related moments of my life hilarious and were likely more unsettled by the fact that I hadn't told them about it immediately than they were by any other part of that experience. *Yeah, yeah, you contemplated wiping your butt with dental floss, but how dare you hold on to this precious gem of a shit story all to yourself for six entire years? Do you not love us anymore?*

I am measurably more comfortable with myself now than I was at eight or as a sophomore in high school. I'm starting to hit the point in my life where telling people embarrassing things I've done (and continue to do) doesn't completely ruin me. I definitely still have pangs of guilt for things I did in middle school that only I remember. I still play that fun game where I try to fall asleep and my brain is like, "Would now be a good time to hyper-analyze a bad presentation you gave in college or no?" I'm also starting to realize that becoming comfortable with myself and finding comfort in those around me is *way* easier than trying to hold in something my body wants to let out. You can learn how to accept yourself and how to find people who will accept you as you are.

You can't learn how to not diarrhea yourself. If you could, I wouldn't have mistrusted a fart in a Lowe's. When that happened, I immediately told Riley. His response was to laugh and KEEP SHOPPING. Again, it was an uneventful occurrence. A few weeks later, I texted my sister about how I'd shit myself, and she immediately called me to verbally berate me for not telling her sooner. I'm lucky to have found people who love me, shit and all.

DAILY AFFIRMATIONS
FOR MY SISTER

Hi, Ana. I wrote this for you. If you, reading this, are not my sister, that's okay too. You can just imagine you are her, something I think would make the world a more compassionate, bizarre, and overall better place.

Let me start by saying: you are allowed to say nice things to yourself. Aloud. In the mirror. I know it feels strange and silly in the moment, but afterward, it feels good. We spend all day secretly telling ourselves mean and nasty things we'd never say to our internet nemesis. We are the devil on our own shoulders hissing, "You probably look stupid right now" and "Remember that time you peed your pants in high school?" We are the voice inside our own head, anxiously pacing in front of a mental corkboard of Post-it notes and red string like, "Everything you've ever said . . . it all leads back to being bad!" You should tell yourself some nice things every once in a while or, if you can manage it, all the time.

If you're feeling stuck or get sick of telling yourself "Good hair, me!" here are some suggestions for things you can say when you want to give your brain a sweet little treat. If you say them aloud, change every "you" to "I." Or read them as is, doing an impression of my voice and pretending I'm telling them to you. If you do the latter, make me sound cool and British, okay?

You are worthy and deserving of a right swipe.

In fact, you are better than a right swipe. Maybe you should delete Tinder altogether. I know how people's Tinder minds work. I, too, was once a Tinderer. The idea of you having to suffer through profiles of shirtless strangers holding some big fish that I'm assuming they . . . fucked?, listing "music" as a whole entire interest, makes me hulk all the way out. (You like music? Really? Do you also like transportation and breathing? Grow up and specify a genre, a musical instrument, or a Beyoncé era.) The thought of a man whose entire personality is having been to Machu Picchu once in middle school swiping through your photos, thinking he can pass judgment on *you*, makes me want to march right up to Silicon Valley and call all of their mothers. You don't need dating apps. You are worthy and deserving of a rom-com meet-cute.

Remember to feed your spirit.

Your spirit gets hungry, and I heard she likes gooey brownies with frosting, big glasses of kombucha, and salty snacks when she least expects it. I know I sound like a Snickers commercial, but sometimes when we feel particularly angry or sad or frustrated, we're just a little hungry. That applies to everyone, but us in particular. We've seen each other in a 3 p.m. tizzy, running around like a headless chicken squawking, "I feel weird. Do you feel weird? Why do I feel weird?!" A well-timed bagel with cream cheese can save a life. (Our own, sure, but mostly the people around us who have to deal with our very real hanger.) Oh, also you should meditate or whatever.

You radiate kindness.

You are like some kind of radioactive bug who is also super nice. It's the sort of disease I wish were contagious. Your kindness is my most and least favorite thing about you. Most, for obvious reasons. Least because of how it lets you give the benefit of the doubt to noticeably terrible people. People like coworkers who say rude things to your face and white college boys with dreads. These people needn't benefit from your doubt.

If I were a better person, this is where I'd say you're doing a good job killing them with kindness. You're crushing the whole "murder them with your radioactive kindness rays" thing. Burn niceness holes into their skin with your gentle touch. Give them whatever the compassionate form of scabies would be.

You are LIGHT. You are LOVE. You are LAUGH. You are LIVE. You are LIPSTICK. You are LLAMA. You are LINDA. You are LIGHTNING. You are "LUCKY" by Britney Spears (2000). Those are all the L words I can think of right now LOL.

Oh, I forgot "LOL."

You don't need to sweat the small stuff.

And even if you wanted to, you couldn't because you don't really sweat that much. I only hold that against you a little bit. I don't understand how I got all the sweaty, hairy genes and you got the "my BO smells like maple syrup" genes.

You can and you will and you have.

Every time you think you can't do a thing you need to do, you somehow, eventually, find yourself on the other side of it. If you woke up one morning and thought, "I bet I could create the next big plant-based milk," you'd have some dandelion milk or smushed-up-acorn milk by the end of the day. That kindness bug you have keeps you from using these powers for evil. Although, "dandelion milk" certainly does seem like its own kind of torture.

You do not need to live in comparison.

This is because everyone else sucks except for you. That's that on that.

You are enough.

Too much even. I've always been a little envious of that. You've always known how to grow and flourish, to turn your branches to the sun, to take up space in a way that is also welcoming. You're like a tree. A tree with boobs.

You are your own superhero.

Are we the only two people in the world who just . . . don't really care about superhero franchises? People always want to talk about how *Avengers* movies are the greatest crossover events in cinematic history, like Disney Channel didn't air "That's So Suite Life of Hannah Montana" in 2006, a television episode that featured Raven-Symoné, Miley Cyrus, and two entire Sprouse twins. If we absolutely *had* to be superheroes, you'd be Mary-Kate and I'd be Ashley.

You are whole.

You've got a head and a body and a heart (organ) and heart (spiritual). You are a whole entire being. You are a complete person, in this sense, but you're far from finished. Please read this part twice: once, with loving eyes and generous big sister energy. Then, read it again, but this time say it like it's an insult, just to keep you balanced.

You are hole.

:)

You have the power to create change.

In that sense, I do need you to break this twenty for me, thanks. (If you were here, this is where you'd laugh condescendingly. I will pause for your obligatory and rude laughter.) I want you to know that you are never stuck. If a job, a person, a situation is hurting more than it is helping, if it is draining more than fulfilling, you can leave. You can go. You can be like, "Oh, sorry, my sister is actually calling right now," and get the fuck out of there.

You can do anything you put your mind to.

If you pressed your little bean into the ground, a bountiful harvest would grow. If you pushed your noggin into a notebook, it would turn into a novel. If you set it on the dining room table, the table would come to life. Your mind is magic, and I do mean that in the most literal *Frosty the Snowman* kind of way.

You are loved unconditionally.

Specifically by me. I've told you before that if you said you murdered someone, my reaction would be, "I bet it was for a good reason. I'll go get some bleach." Once, Riley said he didn't like Doritos, and I started looking up how fast I could get a divorce in Kansas.

You deserve goodness.

When I think of the things I want for you, every single thing I wish and hope and dream for you, I want to puke. It's kind of like how when you think about space too hard it makes you nauseous. I love you as big as the universe. I love you as deep as the ocean. I love you as wide as my eyes get every time you're like, "Want to see all the tonsil stones I just pulled out of my mouth?"

You will never join a rec league.

Or an improv team. These are less affirmations than they are demands, but they're for your own good.

FATHER MIA

One of my favorite games growing up, among Guess Who? and Scrabble and making my siblings drink offensive concoctions I created in the blender, was Church: Catholic Edition. If you don't know anything about Catholics, they're the ones with all the kneeling and sitting and standing and chant-like prayers and spooky singing and swinging balls of incense and repression and hidden sex abuse. The way you play Church is relatively simple. First, you start by being born into a family that goes to church and being raised in a community that indoctrinates you into Christianity. I guess that part isn't that simple.

Then, after years of seeing old men lead Mass every Sunday, singing off-key and raising their hands at certain parts like an air traffic controller, you think, "I could do that." So you make your family sit in the spare bedroom, dim the lights, have your mom light a candle, and you lead Mass.

When I played Church, I'd drape a blanket I made in Sunday school over my shoulders as a makeshift vestment. The blanket had different Catholic imagery stitched on—a cross, a tabernacle, a Bible, probably a dove or a lamb for good measure—and was signed in fabric marker by all the other second-graders in my CCD class. "CCD" stands for "Confraternity of Christian Doctrine" and is an extremely Latin-sounding way to be like, "You kids are going to accept Christ, got it?"

After I set the altar (a circular side table that wobbled a little) and dressed in my priestly blanket-robe, my family would file into the room and greet me as I'd requested. "Hello, Father Mia," my dad would say. "Hello, Dad," I'd say back with no hint of irony. I had no interest in preaching or giving a homily or reading passages from the Bible, all the boring parts of a Catholic Mass. I'm sure I had them sing my favorite hymn ("On Eagle's Wings," a song specifically for funeral masses), but then we'd get right to the good part of Church: Communion.

First Communion is one of the seven sacraments in Catholicism alongside other milestones like baptism, marriage, and confirmation. Children typically receive their First Communion in second grade—around the time I started playing Church a lot. Having your First Communion is a big deal in the Catholic Church. You spend your CCD classes leading up to it by practicing how to walk up the church aisle, how to hold your hands in preparation for the host (the circular wafer that tastes like crunchy air), what the priest or Eucharistic minister would say when you got to the front of the line and they held the host up to you ("The body of Christ"), what you would say in return ("Amen"). I learned the call-and-response of receiving Communion before I knew about long division, persuasive essays, the Trail of Tears, where babies come from, or what puberty is.

Though I'm sure it was part of the curriculum, I don't remember talking about *why* Communion is such a big to-do. I assume my seven-year-old brain processed it as, "We get to eat Jesus and eating Jesus is, I'm guessing, important?" I was much more focused on the fact that I'd get gifts, a cake that said, "Congratulations on your First Communion, Amelia," and the chance to wear a fancy white dress.

My First Communion dress was passed down from my mom. It was the same dress she wore on her First Communion. It had lace detailing, beaded accents, and came with matching gloves and a veil. Yes, a child-sized veil. For girls, First Communion attire is like a bigger version of a baptismal gown and a smaller version of a wedding dress because Catholics aren't concerned with subtly. Boys were expected to wear suits and ties, like child grooms or baby businessmen. I don't remember if we walked down the church aisle paired up girl-boy during our actual First Communion, but it would be very on-brand for the whole experience if we did.

The Communion I administered to my family while playing Church involved much less formal wear. Before my at-home service started, I'd find some thin crackers in our house, preferably a rice cracker but a Ritz would also do. "The body of Christ," I'd say to each member of my family as they reached the front of the Communion line. (My Communion had no age restrictions so my younger brother and sister could participate.) I'd lift the salty snack above my bowl, blessing it with my grubby little seven-year-old hands. "Amen," they'd respond.

Then, I'd grab the glass of "wine" I'd prepared earlier as well. "The blood of Christ," I'd say, holding a cup of grape juice or water I'd died red-purple with food coloring. "Amen," they'd say. After all five of my parishioners made it through the Communion line, service would be done.

Like most kids, I also grew up playing School and House and Musical. Musical is where I'd write a musical and make my siblings perform it alongside me. There are hours of home video footage of me saying, "And NOW I preSENT to YOU" as an introduction to something I'd written or choreographed or reimagined for me and my three siblings. Some might have called me "precocious"; others may have said I was "bossy." Both were coded ways to say "annoying."

Just as playing Musical never led to starring roles in high school shows, being Father Mia did not carry over into my adulthood. I never wanted to be a nun, one of the few leadership opportunities for women in the church. I didn't get married in the Catholic Church. I no longer would even identify myself as "Christian," something I know my parents take personally.

Though I haven't been to church on my own in years, the many rites and rituals of Catholicism are hard to break and shake off. I know to genuflect before entering a church pew, a situation I encounter so seldom my knees crack when I do so. I know the sign of the cross as reflexively as my left and right. In addition to all the *Amen*s and *And with your spirit*s Catholicism is known for, we have a fun thing called Confession. That's where you tell a priest every sin you've ever done, the priest tells you to do a certain number of prayers in a specific order, and then you are forgiven. Another game I'd play with my parents was Can You Even Get Forgiven for That? That was where I'd list things I knew to be Very Bad (murder, stealing, lying about turning in your social studies assignment even though you didn't) and ask if even those sins could be absolved. The answer, to my surprise, was almost always "yes."

First Reconciliation is where you give a confession to a priest for the first time. It is another one of the seven sacraments in Catholicism and happens when you are in fourth grade, a normal time for a kid to have done a shitload of sins. Unlike First Communion, this sacrament required no gown, just nice "church" clothes.

For our First Reconciliation, we didn't go into the confessional booth like you see in movies. There were no dimly lit cubicles, ominous shadows, or partitions with curtains or cross-shaped patterns. Instead, we waited in pews before being called into a spare room of the church I'd never noticed before. It was basically a small conference room, down the hall from where we had Sunday service. The room had one round table, a couple of chairs, and that gross yellow lighting you'd expect from an old church conference room. The only decoration was probably a crucifix on the wall.

One by one, my classmates were called into the conference room to confess their sin(s) to Father Mike, our church's priest.* When it got to my turn, I walked silently into the room and took my seat at the table. Father Mike greeted me, after a quick glance to the name tag we'd been asked to wear. He asked what I wanted to confess and I sat there silent. In the way teachers prep their students to come up with questions to ask a guest speaker, our CCD teachers had asked that we come prepped with some ideas for sins we'd done. I was nine. The worst thing I'd done was get bangs.

"You have siblings, don't you?" Father Mike said as I tried to rack my brain for any confession-worthy sin I'd done. I'm not sure if he knew I was one of four because our church was rela-

---

* Did you know every church has a Father Mike? If yours didn't, perhaps *you* were the Father Mike.

tively small or because our church was Catholic, but Father Mike was pretty comfortable functioning under the assumption that I was not an only child. I nodded.

"Do you ever fight with your siblings?" he asked, trying to get me to say something, anything remotely sinful. I nodded again, a half-truth. My siblings and I bickered as you'd expect four kids each two years apart to do, but we never really fought. At least, not in a way that I thought was necessary of holy forgiveness.

After some convincing on his part, we decided that would be my "confession." I don't remember if he had me recite any prayers or ask for forgiveness. I only remember thinking, "I just lied during my First Reconciliation. Maybe I can ask for forgiveness for that next time."

As far as I recall, I got no post-confession gifts. I received no cake decorated to say, "Good job on telling that adult male stranger your deepest, darkest secrets, Mia!" It was a significantly more somber experience than drinking Jesus's blood for the first time.

Recently, my parents gave me a box of things I still had at their house: pictures from a disposable camera I'd taken one summer in high school, old diaries, a collection of CDs that included Michelle Branch and a bootleg version of Simple Plan's debut album, and various certificates for my Catholic sacraments.

Despite going through almost every one of the sacraments, attending church weekly from birth until I was eighteen, and going to weekly religion classes since I'd gone to school, I never really thought about being Catholic. It was just part of my identity in the way my hair is dark brown and one of my feet is slightly bigger than the other.

The first time I really thought about religion was during a conversation with my first serious boyfriend. He asked if I thought of myself as Christian, and I said "yeah" reflexively, matter-of-factly, even. As if he'd just asked if we lived in the United States or whether I wanted pizza. "So, you believe Jesus is your lord and savior and died for your sins?" he said, not condescendingly or antagonistically. He was genuinely curious. Out of context, it seems like a wild statement—that someone lived thousands of years ago just to die for your inevitable nature of fucking up. I thought Jesus seemed cool and smart, but I didn't know if I *like* liked him, you know?

From that point, I started realizing pretty quickly that I really didn't know much about Catholicism besides its rules and regulations. (No sex unless you're married, no abortion for anyone ever, divorce is pretty bad but ugh okay fine you can be forgiven for it.) I never thought about being Catholic in terms of what I believed to be true about myself or others or humanity as a whole. It took such a simple question for me to undo a lifetime of *I believe*s and *I do*s. It took someone asking me the question point-blank to realize I knew almost nothing about this religion I'd spent twenty-two years "practicing," let alone anything about any religion outside of Christianity.

My religious reckoning was pretty undramatic. I didn't go talk to a priest or seek out religious counsel. I didn't panic-google "what religion even am I." I didn't feel like I needed to reevaluate all my core beliefs because I didn't *really* believe anything. And the very basic things I did believe (e.g., be good; don't, like, kill anyone) felt separate from my religion.

I still go to church when I'm home for the holidays because I like being there with my family. I still get comfort from saying prayers my parents would recite to us every night as kids. They're rhythmic and soothing and familiar. Some people can still recite stats from baseball cards or facts about horses they learned as children. I still have all the words to the rosary memorized.

Sometimes my head still bows reflexively to say grace before eating, as if I need to bless the box of Goldfish crackers I'm about to do something completely unholy to. This is the body and blood of Growing Up and Out of the Catholic Church, I suppose. To which I will say, Amen.

CAN I BE A GOOD GIRL WHILE STILL GETTING FUCKED UP?

I didn't drink in high school. I didn't do drugs in college. I can count the number of times I've smoked a cigarette on one finger. If you're wondering whether I'd be chill on anything harder than alcohol or pot, the answer is one time, in elementary school, I ate a mint leaf and thought I was going to die.

In first or second grade, our class took a field trip to a local nature center. We were led on a tour through a wooded trail, our guide pointing out certain plants for us to take note of and which animals lived where. I was toward the back of the line, partially paying attention to our tour guide, mostly paying attention to Michael A., who was walking a few paces in front of me and happened to be my second biggest crush at the time. (Matt B. was number one, but he wasn't on the field trip. So Michael A. had to do.) We stopped for a second as the guide gestured to a tree and relayed, I'm assuming, some tree facts. Again, I was very preoccupied with the back of Michael A.'s head.

The girl I was standing next to nudged me, pointed down to a plant growing from the ground, and said, "You should eat that."

I distinctly remember her pointing at a mint plant. I knew mint was a food flavor, but I'd never seen it in leaf form. I also knew it probably wasn't the best idea to eat strange plants on a field trip or perhaps ever. Still, the girl just kept staring at me like, "I'm only going to ask you once." So I did what she said. I ate a leaf from the plant.

No less than thirty seconds later, our tour guide gave us a friendly reminder to "please don't touch or eat the plants! Hands to ourselves! Thank you!" I immediately froze. I still don't know if she saw me eat the plant or just had a prescient enthusiasm, but I felt like I'd been caught.

I've always been scared of getting in trouble. When encountering anyone with any form of authority (teachers, parents, crossing guards, Walgreens employees rearranging the discounted lube), I still hear both my parents angry-whispering, "Behave!" In school, I did what teachers asked when they asked me to do it. I turned in homework assignments on time. I wrote essays with thesis statements I thought my teacher would agree with rather than my personal interpretation of *Great Expectations*. "Dickens's novel is important and good and I definitely read it and did not just re-watch the episode of PBS's *Wishbone* where they depict Miss Havisham's wedding dress catching fire and Wishbone, the titular Jack Russell, saving her with a tablecloth. In this essay, I will . . ."

I followed directions. I always listened. I grew up thinking that being obedient and being good were one and the same.

I spent the rest of the nature center field trip thinking I was going to die either of plant poisoning or shame. *The tour guide said not to touch or eat anything,* I thought, *because it could make you sick and dead and your parents will hate you and Michael*

A. won't sit by you on the bus ride home because you'll smell like death and mint leaves.

As I got older, I knew I couldn't handle any major intoxicant if I had that bad of a trip off a dessert garnish. I didn't feel pressured to drink before I wanted to, probably because I made it abundantly clear that I was a "good kid" and good kids don't drink.

Because our town was relatively small and high schoolers can't keep their mouths shut, word about who was throwing a party on the weekend got around quickly. There was one kid in my class who threw parties at his parents' house a lot. If this was a coming-of-age movie, he would be played by a store-brand Dave Franco and that casting would be generous. My classmate, who we'll call Dave, was friendly when we crossed paths at Sunday school, though we didn't run in the same social circle.

Who you are in high school feels like such a big deal when you're in high school. And at the beginning of college. And while thinking about your teen years in hindsight. Whenever people talk about how little high school matters, I think about a story my grandma once told me. At her fiftieth high school reunion, a classmate came up to her and apologized for how he'd treated her when they were teenagers. A kind and strange gesture, fifty years overdue. I asked my grandma if she remembered what he'd done or said. "Not really," she told me, but she did remember him as "kind of mean" because of how he'd made her feel. For every "Everyone will get over it, no one will remember," we each have one of these stories.

Who we thought ourselves to be in high school both doesn't matter at all while also explaining so much. I was not part of the "cool" group in high school. Being cool was reserved for hot sporty girls named Lindsay and hot party girls who got in trouble for wearing shirts that said "EAT ME" to school. I was friends with kids who were good at school, good at following directions, good at not getting in trouble. I wanted teachers and parents to like me. I was the kid who friends' moms would call "the marrying type," which is not much consolation when all you want is for someone to, for the love of God, make out with you already.

While I was never invited to a party at Dave's, I did go a few times, in a sense. I imagined these parties to be full of people drinking out of red cups and dancing in a backyard lit with Tiki torches. I assumed there was a lot of suggestive hair flipping and grinding, the latter of which our principal warned we'd be banned from doing at high school dances if we didn't cool it. I pictured the whole scene playing out in slow motion with thumping bass, girls *woo*-ing, and boys jumping into an in-ground pool. I have no idea if Dave even had a pool.

When I say I "went to these parties," what I mean is one of my friends (who also didn't drink) and I made a habit of driving past Dave's house on Friday nights to see whose cars we recognized. "Nick, Matt, both Lindsays," we'd say to each other, taking roll call of which friends we assumed were getting wasted in Dave's parents' basement. We'd drive slowly enough so we could make out who was there but not so slowly that someone might spot us. I was neither cool nor chill in high school.

Though I'm sure by now you think I'm a complete narc, I never told my parents or called the cops. Our intention was not to rat anyone out to some authority figure. *We* were the authority figure. We got to pass all the judgment we wanted, talking about how dumb and bad everyone there was and how smart and good we were. "I can't believe they think that's cool," we'd say, peering through the windows of my friend's Toyota Corolla, leaning our seats all the way back because we thought it'd be more inconspicuous. "So lame," we'd scoff, ducking down anytime we thought we saw a headlight.

High school me wasn't sober in an "I'm straight-edge and that rocks my socks off! Red Ribbon Week for life!" kind of way. It was more of an "I don't drink so I'm a good kid. If you drink, that means you're a bad kid, and I will think about that joyfully when I'm a successful businesswoman with lots of blazers" kind of thing. Because I based so much of who I was on *not* doing something, the natural next step was to make assumptions about anyone who did that thing. Not drinking = good, smart, Mom and Dad will be proud, teachers will give you awards, success, money, profit. Drinking = bad, dumb, flunk out of school, disappoint your family, destroy your future, no money or profit.

Years later, I asked a friend who was cool enough to be invited to Dave's parties what they'd do there. "I don't really remember," he said. "One time, a bunch of people made out in Dave's little sister's castle playhouse." So the reality of the situation was even doper than I imagined.

Toward the end of high school, a bunch of my friends threw a party where they were going to drink for the first time. They didn't tell me and a handful of other people from our friend group about it because they knew we didn't want to drink. It's cool. Again, I did have strong narc vibes.

Somehow though, we got unintentionally invited. When we showed up at the house, our friends started migrating to the kitchen. We realized that not only were they drinking, but they also didn't want to tell us they were drinking. My nondrinking friends and I left in what I'm sure could be described as "a tizzy."

I wasn't upset I'd accidentally gone to "a drinking party" without knowing. That was the made-for-TV teen drama of which I longed to be the star. I was upset they were doing A Thing and didn't tell me about The Thing. Moreover, I was mad that people, who I knew to be "good," could do things I'd been told over and over again were "bad."

I waited until I was pretty much the legal age to start drinking. I drank a little when I was nineteen and twenty, but it was limited to New Year's Eve. Both times I had a total of maybe two shots over the course of the night and spent the rest of the evening going, "I don't think I'm drunk. Do I seem drunk to you? Because I don't really feel drunk. Do you feel drunk? I don't feel drunk," until I got tired and fell asleep.

The first time I got high, I was twenty-four. Riley and I split a couple of old edibles, debating whether their oldness would make them more effective, less effective, or ruin our bodies entirely. If you're going to get high for the first time, I would recommend doing it with someone you like, in a space you feel comfortable, and right before rewatching the Disney Channel original movie *Zenon: Girl of the 21st Century*.

If you're not familiar with *Zenon*, it's the 1999 Kirsten Storms vehicle in which Storms plays a mischievous teen in space. Raven-Symoné plays her best friend. There's a pop star named Proto Zoa. There are futuristic "video phone tablets." It doesn't hold up even a little bit.

If you're not familiar with weed edibles, they make you super high and make the plot to *Zenon* extremely hard to follow. Trying to remember what happened scene to scene was an impossible task. Nothing made sense. Everything was confusing, both in and out of the *Zenon* universe.

I'm not sure whether the experience was good or bad or just . . . an experience. I was both convinced that everything I said was the dumbest thing any person could ever say and every line of *Zenon* was secretly coded poetry. Neither of those things are true.

My rule-following instincts have stuck with me well into adulthood, though I do push boundaries more now than I did as a teen. I get a little drunk on the weekends. I've smoked enough weed to know what my body feels like when it's high without having to say, "I don't think I'm high. Do I seem high to you? Because I don't really feel high. Do you feel high? I don't feel high."

Even still, as an adult, I have this recurring chorus that plays in my head pretty much every time I'm making an even slightly controversial decision, from whether to acknowledge the offensive thing someone said to how I talk to any authority figure to whether I should eat a weed gummy. The chorus goes something like this:

Do what you're told
Do what you're told
Follow the rules so you're a good person
Do what you're fucking told

There were "good kids" who drank in high school and guess what? Some of them became good adults and successful businesspeople with lots of blazers. I'm not immune to the strange cultural pressure to have a good story from a time you were fucked up beyond all repair. I'd be lying if I said I didn't occasionally wonder whether I "missed out" on something by not getting slizzard in high school or college, if I'd be more chill as an adult, if I'd seem cooler or more relatable or more interesting. I'd be doubly lying if I said I didn't have to look up "slizzard" just now.

Ultimately, I'm glad I waited to do the things I wanted to do until I was actually ready to do them. Some rules are fine and necessary and keep us from doing dumb shit when we're still kids. But some rules are made by people who are, at the end of the day, just people. You reach a point when all of a sudden you're a grown person making grown decisions and you have to ask yourself, "What are my choices saying about me, and why am I making those choices?" I'm learning that all my actions can't be to appease some authority figure. *I* am often the authority figure.

I wish I'd realized sooner that obedience isn't all that's required of goodness, that casting other people as bad didn't automatically make me good. Most importantly, I'm glad I've learned how fucking great Disney Channel movies are while you're high. Better late than never.

CAN I ASK THIS PERSON ABOUT THEIR RACE: A GUIDE

1. Are you asking about someone running an athletic race?
   - If YES, go to number 11
   - If NO, go to number 2

2. Why do you want to ask this person about their race?
   - "Because I can't tell what race they are and I'm curious": go to number 5
   - "For government census reasons": go to number 3
   - "Because I'm trying to flirt and this is how I try to flirt": go to number 69 ;)

3. Really?
   - If NO, go to number 4

4. Is it actually just because you can't tell what race they are and you're curious?
   - If YES, go to number 5

5. Do you know this person?

   - "Yes, we know each other": go to number 7

   - "Yeah, we're acquaintances": go to number 6

   - "Yep, I've been standing near them for, like, three full minutes": go to number 6

6. You're talking about a stranger, aren't you?

   - For "Yeah," go to number 12

7. What's your pants size?

   - For "Huh?" go to number 8

8. I'm just curious.

   - For "I don't think this is how this works," go to number 9

9. No, but I think I know someone who's the same pants size as you.

   - For "We weren't even talking about pants," go to number 10

10. Was race relevant to whatever conversation you were having?

    - If YES, go to number 13

    - If NO, go to number 12

11. Yeah, sure.

    What an oddly specific thing to consult a choose-your-own-adventure-style guide about. Carry on, my friend.

12. Nope. Doesn't seem relevant or necessary to ask about this person's race.

    Carry on thinking about more important things, like how dogs have been to space or how dust is mostly skin.

13. If the context seems appropriate, okay.

    However, that person might not feel comfortable sharing, and that's also okay. I promise you, this is probably not the first time this person has been asked about their race. Now you can talk about more important things, like how dogs have been to space or how dust is mostly skin.

69. Kindly go fuck yourself. ;)

ALL RISE FOR THE
HONORABLE MIA MERCADO

You ever see something that makes you want to go full Sonia Sotomayor? You ever hear a comment that makes you want to call for order in the court of life and channel that Ruth Bader Ginsburg energy? You ever see an episode of *Judge Judy* and think, "Fuck, I'd love to hit a gavel"? Me too. So, today, as I do every day in private, I will be passing judgment on the cases that come across my desk. Or, more likely, things that simply come into my periphery and make me say, "Not in my court."

I am Judge Mia Mercado presiding over this proverbial courtroom. Though you cannot see it, I am wearing a robe. It is comfy, cozy, and yes, okay, it is just a Snuggie. Our courtroom's bailiff is also me but a version of me that is jacked like Dwayne "The Rock" Johnson, which brings me to my first case.

Case #1: Me vs. the People Who Leave "The Rock" out of Dwayne "The Rock" Johnson's Full Name

I know he's trying to rebrand as an actor, but I will never stop smelling what Dwayne "The Rock" is cooking. He did so much for media representation of people who can raise one of their eyebrows, of whom I am one. I cannot look at current Dwayne "The Rock" Johnson without picturing his late '90s sideburns that reached halfway down his jawline. You are not allowed to have that body type, call yourself "The Rock," and then just *stop*.

We can acknowledge the person he is becoming ("Dwayne Johnson") while still paying homage to his, and our, history ("The Rock"). It is so ordered.

Cases #2–6: The Food Files

KIT KATS: The proper way to eat a Kit Kat is to break it apart into individual bars as the chocolate gods intended. Biting into a Kit Kat whole, leaving an anarchistic tooth mark across all four bars, is a hate crime against me specifically. Do you want to be the perpetrator of a hate crime?

NOT LIKING DORITOS: Riley recently told me he doesn't "like" Doritos, which I didn't realize was even an option. That's like saying you'd rather not breathe oxygen or live on planet Earth. Sorry, but you're a human. Humans are programmed to eat Doritos.

"PIZZA" FLAVORING: The Ruling? It's bad. Artificial pizza flavoring always tastes like someone whispered "pizza" into a pile of puke and mixed in some tomato paste to cover it up. We need to stop asking if we *can* flavor-blast things and start asking if we *should*. Particularly when that flavor being blasted is something as sacrilegious as fake pizza. It is an affront to our country, our creator, and real pizza.

BEING RUDE TO RESTAURANT STAFF: People who make a show of whether or not they're going to tip well, being condescending to a waiter, or making an intentionally big, crumbly mess of everything should be sentenced to a life of only getting to eat pizza-flavored things. You want fries? They're going to be dusted with a pizza-flavored powder. Did someone order the pizza-flavored beignet? No? Well, you snapped rudely at the hostess and now your delicious dessert is an acidic, powdered-sugar-covered pizza pocket.

SAYING YOU'RE "JUST NOT A SWEETS PERSON": First of all, how dare you. What did ice cream ever do to you? Were you personally victimized by a chocolate bar? Have you never tried cake? I don't understand how someone can say they're not a "sweets person" like they've tried *every single sweet* in existence? If you tell me you are not one for sweets, I will spend the next hour or two or the rest of infinity listing a sweet and seeing if you like it. Coffee cake? Chocolate graham crackers? Perchance a peach cobbler? I can keep going and, legally, I am obligated to.

Case #7: Microaggressions vs. Me

People (read: "white people") are often worried I'm going to pass judgment on them. If I had a dollar for every time someone has asked whether I'd judge them before they were about to say a thing that was definitely going to be racist, I would have enough money to hire an intern to field those questions for me. It's a strange balance to want to help people learn while also trying not to absorb every stupid thing everyone's stupid brain wants to say with their stupid mouths. But in this Courtroom of Implicit Bias, I am in no place to pass judgment.

Once, while talking about race to two coworkers (both of whom aren't white), I relayed a story about the only time I'd been mistaken as white. It was when I'd gotten pulled over for speeding a few years ago.

On the ticket, next to my name, my address, and the amount of my fine, there was a box that said "RACE." It was filled in with the word "White." My license doesn't designate my race. I certainly didn't roll down my window and say, "Greetings, Officer. It's just me, one White Woman going a little too quickly on her way to work!" But the police officer marked my race down as "white" on my ticket anyway.

When I finished the story, my coworkers just stared at me for a moment. Then they talked about the times cops had followed them around department stores, how they notice they get pulled over more when they wear their hair a certain way, how police officers have made a point to ask the group of white friends they're with whether those white friends were "being bothered."

My white-adjacent privilege as a lighter-skinned, half-Asian person really jumped the fuck out. While I can see the ways in which the world "others" me clear as day, I'm often still blind to the insidious ways I benefit from anti-blackness, anti-brownness, the fucked-up idea of the "model minority," etc.

Look, everyone says dumb things, myself very much included. If I actively passed judgment on every dumb thing everyone said to or at or near me, smacking them in the head with my metaphoric gavel, I'd explode. Still, it shouldn't be my job to teach you how to be kind to me.

It would do the world some good to be sentenced to feeling a bit more empathy. To set up their own privilege checkpoints, identifying their blind spots instead of waiting for someone to do it for them. To be reminded that—instead of explaining why the racist thing they said isn't *actually* racist, how they didn't *mean* for it to be racist, or how they *can't* be racist because they always tip their Asian nail technician really well—they have the right to remain silent. Also, if one more person asks where I'm "really" from, I will do a citizen's arrest on them.

Case #8: Current Me vs. 2013 Me Who Got Noticeably Bad Bangs

Like every woman in her late-twenties, I have dabbled in getting bangs. Here an excerpt from the actual court transcript from one case of particularly bad bangs.

> **JUDGE MIA:** Let me start by asking three simple questions: Why? Why? And furthermore, whywhywhywhy whyWHY?!

> **2013 MIA:** Aren't you supposed to be impartial?

> **JUDGE MIA:** I apologize, my bangs bias is showing. Current Ms. Mercado, present your argument.

> **CURRENT MIA:** Your honor, she knew something was wrong the second the stylist left her hair parted to one side. He grabbed a little chunk from each side and just CUT STRAIGHT ACROSS.

JUDGE MIA: Let the record show the plaintiff turned her fingers into "scissors" and did a snipping motion across the middle of her forehead.

2013 MIA: He said the cowlick would smooth out eventually.

CURRENT MIA: It wasn't a cowlick. It was our natural part!

JUDGE MIA: ORDER! ORDER! The defendant will have her chance to talk in a moment. Please continue, Ms. Mercado.

CURRENT MIA: Thank you, your honor. The cowlick never went away. We tried hair spray, styling mousse, rewetting and blow-drying it. It was just a bad haircut.

JUDGE MIA: Does the defendant have anything to say for herself?

2013 MIA: I wanted a change.

CURRENT MIA: You could have just gotten a trim like a mentally stable person!

2013 MIA: [indistinguishable]

JUDGE MIA: You'll need to speak up. I can barely take you seriously as it is with those bangs. Just remember you are under oath.

2013 MIA: Thank you, your honor. I said that I'd just re-watched *500 Days of Summer*.

CURRENT MIA: BUT WE—

JUDGE MIA: ORDER! ORDER!

CURRENT MIA: Your honor, the evidence is relevant to this particular piece of the testimony.

JUDGE MIA: I'll allow.

CURRENT MIA: Thank you, your honor. You'll see, from this IMDB photo, that we *do not* have remotely the same face shape as Zooey Deschanel and, therefore, could not, under any circumstance, pull off those bangs.

JUDGE MIA: Does the defendant have any point of clarification?

2013 MIA: . . . No, your honor.

CURRENT MIA: Also, she knew he was botching it when he started cutting the hair straight across!

JUDGE MIA: Is this true?

2013 MIA: I mean, yeah. What he was doing didn't seem right, but I was too embarrassed to say anything.

JUDGE MIA: That follows what character witnesses have said. I will ask the plaintiff whether she thinks she would do anything differently, were she to find herself in the same stylist's chair.

CURRENT MIA: I would *never* do something like that.

JUDGE MIA: Interesting. It says here you have a record of not sending food back at a restaurant even when it's not at all close to what you asked for? I also see that once you found a literal fly in your enchilada and you just . . . ate around it. Is that correct?

CURRENT MIA: [indistinguishable]

JUDGE MIA: I just asked that she [gestures to DEFEN-DANT] speak up. Do I need to ask you, too? Now, did you or did you not once eat around an enchilada that shared a plate with an entire dead bug?

CURRENT MIA: . . . Yeah, I did that.

JUDGE MIA: Okay, I've made my decision. 2013 Mia, you've put yourself through enough. As have you, Current Mia. Your punishment will be waiting for these terrible bangs to grow out. Court dismissed.

BAILIFF MIA: Your honor, you have another hearing imme-diately after this.

JUDGE MIA: We got bangs again, didn't we?

Case #9: My Dog vs. Anyone Who Will Not Pet Her

As a self-designated judge, it is both my privilege and my responsi-bility to speak on behalf of those who cannot speak for themselves. My dog, however, is perfectly capable of speaking for herself.

Ava is convinced with all eight pounds of her being that wher-ever she goes, all the people in that space are solely there to meet her. And you know what? She's right. She's a perfectly stinky, stupidly soft, little fluff with a face so cute it should probably be illegal. That's not even parental bias; most everyone who's met Ava says she is adorable. Riley is historically not a dog person (another thing that should be illegal, but I digress), but he took one look at Ava and was like, "Oh, yeah. She's perfect." Ava is change-your-mind, steal-your-man, fuck-up-your-whole-life-but-you'll-allow-it levels of cute.

Ava is constantly running for Dog Mayor of Ava Town, greeting any and all human constituents she crosses paths with. If Riley and I take Ava to a restaurant patio, a park, a drive-through, and any person she sees *doesn't* acknowledge her, she barks at them. It's not an aggressive "Don't fuck with me" bark. It's a sad, desperate "Please, fuck with me, I beg of you" bark. If Ava had her way, she'd sentence the human population to carry her from place to place, claiming squatters' rights on any lap she lands on. I suppose it's only fair retribution for humans inbreeding her kind so much.

Case #10: Me vs. Myself

It's like, *wow*, okay, bitch. You think you know *everything*? You think you *know* everything? *You* think you know everything? Did you miss the whole bangs fiasco? Did you forget when you hid your poop underwear in a woodpile? Remember that time, moments ago, when you realized "one and the same" was not "one IN the same"?

Who the fuck are *you*?

But it's also like, um, remember how you, on your own, changed your whole life around in one summer? Remember how you started taking care of your mental health? Remember how you got married and capably take care of a whole entire dog? Remember how you wrote this book?

Maybe in the mix of feeling strange and stupid, judging ourselves for feeling awkward and out of place, we learn to level out. Maybe we realize that feeling weird is just a standard part of being alive. Maybe, at some point, we all end up normal.

ACKNOWLEDGMENTS

Thank you to my literary agent Monica Odom. This book would not have been possible without your guiding hand, your keen eye for creating a story, and your general badassery.

Thank you to my editorial team, Hilary Swanson and Aidan Mahony, who patiently combed through this book and helped craft each piece into something stupidly perfect and vice versa. You are the co-parenting throuple that book dreams are made of.

Thank you to Judith Riotto for her copyediting prowess and for catching the time I miscredited the year Britney Spears released "Lucky." I never would have lived it down.

Thank you to the teams at HarperOne and HarperCollins for publishing this book even though I am not even a little bit famous and did make you put the word "fingerbang" in print.

Thank you to Emma Allen, Chris Monks, Fiona Taylor, Caitlin Kunkel, Brooke Preston, Carrie Wittmer, Erika W. Smith, and all the editors I've been lucky enough to work with. Your encouragement and guidance fed my gross little ego and in no small part helped make this book possible.

Thank you to Chase Castor for his master photography and for allowing me to live out my Pageant Mom Dreams in a photo

shoot with my dog. Thank you, Kelly Castor, for allowing your beautiful artwork to get a little nasty on my book cover.

Thank you, Camden Hanzlick-Burton and Margaret Hanzlick-Burton, for reading an early version of this book and giving me FaceTime pep talks. You make my heart poop its pants in a good way. Thank you, Valerie Stark, for your expert editorial eye, your comedic sensibilities, and showering me with love and celebratory drinks. Thank you, Rachel Ignotofsky, for championing the things I do and reading what I write, the latter of which is truly the highest compliment. Thank you, Sami, for being cool with me airing our middle school dirty Dollz laundry. I have known you longer than I've known myself.

To my family, thank you and sorry for the part where I said "fingerbang." Mom and Dad, thank you for always supporting the work I want to do, even when that work has been strange or confusing or didn't come with a retirement plan. I love you.

To Zoey, Frankie, and Ana, thank you for just being. I am who I am because of each of you and getting to be your sister is my favorite thing. Labyu!!!

To Riley, something something clever callback to how I love you infinitely. Okay, love me.

ABOUT THE AUTHOR

MIA MERCADO is a writer based in the Midwest. She's originally from Milwaukee and probably pronounces "bag" wrong. Her work has been featured in *The New Yorker*, the *New York Times*, *Washington Post*'s The Lily, *New York* magazine's The Cut, Bustle, *McSweeney's*, and a bottle she threw in the Milwaukee River when she was nine. Mia is pictured here with her dog, Ava, who can't read this book but is perfect nonetheless.